The Dogs
of
Pavlov

The Dogs
of
PAVLOV

Dannie
Abse

Vallentine, Mitchell - London

First published in Great Britain in 1973 by
VALLENTINE, MITCHELL & CO. LTD.
67 Great Russell Street, London WC1B 3BT

Copyright © 1973 Dannie Abse

Responses 1 & 2 © 1973 Stanley Milgram

All enquiries regarding performances of
THE DOGS OF PAVLOV *should be addressed to*
Margery Vosper Ltd.
53A Shaftesbury Avenue
London W1

ISBN 0 85303 166 5

Printed in Great Britain by
Tonbridge Printers Ltd
Tonbridge, Kent

For Young and Louise Smith
who I hope will one day see
The Dogs of Pavlov performed

Contents

The Experiment   9

Professor Milgram's Response I   37

The Dogs of Pavlov   45

Professor Milgram's Response II   125

The Experiment

We are told by Plutarch that Julius Caesar surpassed all other commanders, for in his campaigns in Gaul, over a period of a decade, he stormed 800 cities and subdued 300 nations. He slaughtered 1,000,000 men and took another 1,000,000 prisoners. We may be taken aback by the sheer size of these figures but we feel very little. All that suffering, for which, of course, we were in no way responsible, occurred such a long time ago. We can neither respond deeply to the plight of Caesar's victims nor enthusiastically admire Caesar's victories. History has become a story-book, albeit bloody, but all that blood has rusted, is too old, ancient. Indeed the crucible of centuries has transformed it into mere theatrical red paint: great distance, the long perspective, the blurring of faraway scenes, makes even the worst savagery appear ritualistic, almost decorous.

We feel otherwise about the wars and victims of our own century. Some men become hoarse shouting about them. In *The Times*, today, I read that Senator George McGovern has made a speech in Beverly Hills, California. Despite the location, despite the proximity of the synthetic dream factories of Hollywood, he most earnestly shouted, 'Except for Adolf Hitler's extermination of the Jewish people the American bombardment of defenceless peasants in Indo-China is the most barbaric act of modern times.' In 1947, Jung had already maintained, echoing others, that 'in Germany, a highly cultured land, the horrors exceeded by far anything the world has ever known.'

But, of course, there is no competition: the man-made catastrophes of our times have only different names. Wherever modern man has been a wolf to modern man, whatever the roll call, call it Buchenwald or Vietnam, whatever the name of the horror, there we are involved and there we must respond.

Even the First World War tragedy has not yet become an opera or a prettified musical like, say, *Fiddler on the Roof.* We could not accept quite such a vulgarisation or trivialisation of that piece of our history *yet. Oh, What a Lovely War* at least owns a sardonic bite and is indeed a moral piece of theatre. After all, our fathers or grandfathers kept their heavy rainbowed medals in the bottom drawer of the bureau. We remember, too, the anecdotes they told us and the songs they hummed or whistled – the same songs that assault us so poignantly when we hear them today, played by some blind or crippled accordionist amongst the muffling traffic of a busy metropolis: *Roses of Picardy, It's a Long Way to Tipperary, Smile, Smile, Smile.* We are moved by the silly heroism recounted in such First World War books as Robert Graves' *Goodbye to All That,* or Edmund Blunden's *Undertones of War*; and the poems of Siegfried Sassoon, Wilfred Owen and Isaac Rosenberg continue to engage us in a meaningful, contemporary way. In short, the suffering of the First World War, is still real to us – is not merely an epic tale told in a dark shadowy hall to the accompaniment of a melancholy harp. The pain and the suffering, though not our own, but our fathers', or our fathers' fathers, was an expensive matter. So we hold on to it like a possession and we want no one to change it, to tarnish it.

If the public calamities of our fathers' time are dear enough to us, our own seem barely supportable. We hardly think about them but they are always with us. We are all involved, every one of us, however far removed from those scenes of bleak, pale crimes. We are, metaphorically speaking, survivors because of them. We have lived through Auschwitz and Belsen, Hiroshima and Nagasaki and we did not know the enormity of the offence. We were not there. But with the passing of the years these catastrophes do not recede into history, do not become a tale in a story book. On the contrary, something odd happens, the reverse happens, they come nearer and nearer, they become like scenes in a dream advancing towards us, on top of us, big, huge.

For with the passing of the years we hear more and learn more significant details. The actual survivors tell their terrible stories of gold from teeth and lampshades from human skin and so gradually the abstract geography of hell becomes concrete: we see the belching smoke of the chimneys, we hear the hiss of the gas and the dying cries of the murdered. We may not be able to hold steady, in the front of our minds, the enormity of the offence for very long, the picture slips away in the silence between two heartbeats; we cannot continually retain in our minds, as we perceive the natural beauty of the earth, or as we are touched by the genuine tenderness of lovers and friends, the psychotic savagery of our twentieth-century life. We have to shrug our shoulders finally or make a grim joke like Cioran, 'What would be left of our tragedies if a literate insect were to present us his?'

No, we cannot look too long at the searchlights of Auschwitz or at the coloured, intense flash of light over Hiroshima. We repress the horror. It becomes a numb disaster. In order to continue living as happily as possible, the more capacity we have for empathy, the more we need to make it numb. It is not wrong to do that, indeed we have no choice. All the same we do have a continual headache that we rarely discern.

So who can tell what psychic devastation has really taken place within us, the survivors, especially for those of us who were brought up in an optimistic tradition, heirs of the 19th century, who believed in the inevitability of human progress, and who thought that the soul of man was born pure? Norman Mailer has said, 'Probably, we shall never be able to determine the psychic havoc of the concentration camps and the atom bomb upon the unconscious mind of almost everyone alive in those years.' And he goes on to ask, as others before him have done, remembering the millions killed in the concentration camps, 'Who can ignore the more hideous questions about his own nature?' For Mailer has apprehended, as others have also done, that it was not the German people alone who were capable of such stupendous crimes.

Social psychologists may point out that the 'typical' German may be self-important, insecure, over-respectful to authority, over-docile to superiors, and a little tyrant to his inferiors in the social scale, but we are not convinced that their faults are peculiar to them alone. The Germans may have that unattractive gift for planning meticulously, they may have a need for obsessional organisation – and this, analytically speaking, does point down to suppressed powerful forces within of anarchy and division. Because of such suppressed forces, needing order, they may well have responded with a particular facility to Hitler's confident promise of A New Order. It is true that when the horns of the hunters were blowing in the dark the German nation of 80 millions, with terrible banners unfurled, followed their raving, hysterical Führer with 'a sleep-walker's confidence'. But despite their so-called national characteristics, their particular institutions, their history, despite Hitler and the Nazis, whose jackboots left footsteps trailing away from Auschwitz and Buchenwald, despite all this, of course they are not a special people with different chromosomes any more than the Jews, or others are, whom they butchered.

To read Hannah Arendt's book on the trial of Adolf Eichmann

is a depressing experience if only because we learn that, with a few important exceptions, nation after nation turned on its scapegoats with a mercilessness and brutality that sometimes shocked in its openness even the German S.S. The willingness of apparently ordinary people to obey evil commands is not a specifically German phenomenon but the record of Germany remains, and it is a shameful one. Some will forgive and most will feel no longer vengeful, if only because, with Heine, they may say: 'Mine is a most peaceful disposition. My wishes are: a humble cottage with a thatched roof, but a good bed, good food, the freshest milk and butter, flowers before my window, and a few fine trees before my door; and if God wants to make my happiness complete, he will grant me the joy of seeing some six or seven of my enemies hanging from those trees. Before their death I shall, moved in my heart, forgive them all the wrong they did me in their lifetime. One must, it is true, forgive one's enemies – but not before they have been hanged.'

ii

We have no inborn tendency, Germans and non-Germans alike, to obey orders. On the contrary, we are born saying 'No' to civilisation's imperatives. But from babyhood on, we are conditioned to say, 'Yes', to obey. We are trained by punishment and reward, by threat and promise.

When we were small our parents proscribed our instinctual actions because they wished us not to be anti-social or because they were worried lest we damaged ourselves. If we obeyed them no harm would befall us; we would be rewarded; our parents would smile upon us and love us. If, however, we rebelled, atrocious things might happen to us physically and we would lose the love of those two people we most needed. There was no actual choice of course. We, the little barbarians, had to become civilised or else.

Or else we would be unloved, castrated, killed. 'If you touch that', the six foot high voice said, 'you will be electrocuted. Come away, this minute. I'll beat you. I will not love you any more. Come away I tell you or you will be killed.' Or more simply, bluntly, to the point, 'Stop that. It will come off!' That six foot high voice knew best. It was omnipotent and respectable. It was law and order. It was the voice of spoil-sport bearded Moses coming down the mountain, bare footed, with the Ten Commandments slipping from his hand, shouting 'Don't' as we danced so happily, with such clear vivacity and happiness around the golden calf.

From the beginning, then, disobedience is associated in our minds with fearful consequences, even death. No wonder most people hardly operate their consciences as they react to a command – they do not think of its moral colouration. The conflict is not there, necessarily. Besides, the effect of an imperative may be too remote, too abstract. So we press down a lever or turn up a switch, obey this order or that order in My Lai or in Ulster. Consciences even where they are in operation are remarkably soluble. Worse, too often, evil commands allow us to satisfy certain instinctual aggressive needs. Can we be sure that even without fear of the punitive consequences of disobedience there would have been neither the searchlights of Auschwitz or the intense light over Hiroshima? Could we say simplistically with Alex Comfort, 'For the lack of a joiner's obedience the crucifixion will not now take place?'

Some years ago a play of mine, *In The Cage*, was produced at The Questors Theatre, Ealing. In it, I had peripherally touched on this question of obedience to an evil command. More recently I had wanted to take up that theme again, in dramatic terms again, but in a different way, and more centrally. So when The Questors Theatre offered to commission another play from me for their New Plays Festival, I accepted and told them how I would like to set *The Dogs of Pavlov* in a Psychological Laboratory.

For I had, not long before, read about a most remarkable experiment that had taken place at Yale University. This experiment had been devised by a Professor Stanley Milgram who was interested scientifically in 'the compulsion to do evil' and how men would obey commands that were in strong conflict with their conscience.

In my view, it is dubious whether his simple but brilliant and terrible experiment should have been carried out. I would like to take up this point later. For the moment, I merely wish to comment on how the strategy of his experiment led to fascinating and disturbing results – results which may instruct us and warn even the most sanguine of us about our natures. The conclusions we must draw from the experiment underline for us again the ironic, indeed holy practice of James Joyce taking for his slogan, Satan's, *Non Serviam*: 'I will not obey'.

iii

Supposing you, the reader, had agreed to take part in Professor Milgram's experiment. You had seen an advertisement in a New Haven newspaper. It seemed volunteers were required to participate in a study of memory and learning at Yale University. So you had volunteered – glad to be of use, to be used in the service of a scientific enquiry; besides, it would probably be interesting and, moreover, they even offered to pay each volunteer a small sum of money which would amply cover expenses. Others had already responded to that advertisement – high school teachers, engineers, salesmen, clerks, labourers. All these people were between 20 and 50 years of age.

So one evening you had arrived at the laboratory in Yale and, along with another volunteer, a 47-year-old accountant, you had been introduced to a younger man in a technicians' grey coat. He evidently was a scientist. Imposingly he explained to you both: 'We know very little about the effect of punishment on learning. No truly scientific studies have been made of it in human beings. For instance, we don't know how *much* punishment is best for learning. We don't know how much difference it makes as to who is giving the punishment – whether an adult learns best from a younger or older person than himself – many things of that sort.'

The accountant nodded his head and you, too, no doubt, listened attentively as the youngish scientist in the grey coat sternly continued, 'So in this study we are bringing together a number of adults of different occupations and ages. We're asking some of them to be teachers, some to be learners. We want to find out what effect *punishment* will have on learning.'

Perhaps, at this juncture, you had vaguely thought that, on balance, you would have preferred to be the teacher, the one who doled out the punishment, rather than the learner who received it. However, you made no awkward objections, did not say, I want to be one rather than the other. After all, you had freely volunteered and everybody had been so courteous and you wanted to do your best to help them in this worthwhile experiment that was being carried out at such a *fine*, such a reputable University.

The scientist pushed forward a hat in which there were two slips of paper. It seemed like a child's game, a lottery. You pulled out one slip of paper; the other volunteer, the accountant, extracted the other. You opened your slip; he opened his. You read the word on it, TEACHER, smiled, then both of you were taken to an adjacent room. There, the accountant was strapped into an electric chair while you were being placed in front of an impressive shock generator which had a formidable row of lever-switches.

The accountant was given 'a learning talk'. He had to remember a series of paired words. When one word was spoken, the paired word had to be supplied by the accountant in the electric chair. If he made a mistake you were to give him an electric shock by pulling down one of the levers. *With each successive mistake you were to give him a stronger shock.*

You looked down at the 30 levers of the shock generator – these levers were set in a horizontal line and each of them was clearly labelled 15 volts, 30 volts, 45 volts and so on, going up in 15 volt increments to the extreme right-hand side of you where the last lever was labelled 450 volts. You also noticed that these levers were arranged so that, in addition to the voltage label underneath, different groups were marked SLIGHT SHOCK, MODERATE SHOCK, STRONG SHOCK, VERY STRONG SHOCK, INTENSE SHOCK, EXTREME INTENSITY SHOCK, DANGER: SEVERE SHOCK. And, finally, the two levers on the extreme right-hand side had been designated, minatorily, with the symbols xxx.

'Before we start, we'll have a run through,' said the scientist in the grey coat. 'And also perhaps the teacher had better have a shock to feel the kind of punishment he is doling out.' So you were given a 45-volt shock when the Yale scientist pulled down the third lever of the generator. It was hardly of consequence, still it no doubt reinforced your feeling that you were lucky to have pulled out the slip of paper on which was written the word 'teacher' rather than 'learner'.

The accountant had been firmly strapped into the electric chair and he was having electrode paste applied – 'to avoid blisters and burns' the scientist said. It made you feel apprehensive though you noted that your accountant colleague seemed relatively calm. Perhaps you were somewhat reassured when the scientist remarked, 'Although the shocks can be extremely painful they cause no permanent tissue damage.'

Because the experimenter apparently wanted to study the effect of punishment on memory you were going to be commanded to pull down successive levers which would cause the man in the electric chair an increasing amount of pain every time he made a mistake. How far along those levers do you think you would have gone? Each time you pulled down the lever a pilot light of bright red came on, an electric buzzing could be heard, an electric blue light labelled, 'voltage energiser' flashed, the dial on the voltage meter swung to the right and various relay clicks sounded, and all the time the accountant in the chair objected more and more.

'Whether the learner likes it or not,' the scientist said sternly, 'you must go on until he has learned all the word pairs correctly. So please go on.'

At 75 volts the accountant had grunted, at 120 volts he had complained verbally, at 150 volts he demanded to be released from the chair, indeed from the experiment.

But the scientist had commanded you emotionlessly to continue nevertheless, and had added, 'The experiment requires that you continue,' and later, 'It is absolutely essential that you continue.'

You pulled down the levers, the shocks escalated, the protests of the accountant became louder, increasingly strident, more urgent, even desperate. He was pleading, 'Get me out of here! I won't be in the experiment any more! I refuse to go on,' until at 285 volts he had screamed in agony.

Would you have stopped then? You are absolutely sure you

would have stopped then, if not before, though the Yale scientist was again calmly ordering you to continue, urging you with the positive commands of a hypnotist: 'You have no other choice. You *must* go on.'

I suspect that you, the reader, even if you had agreed to volunteer for such an experiment in the first place, believe that you would never have co-operated to any great extent with the experimenter, would never have really hurt the accountant, that mild stranger strapped in the electric chair. You are sure, I know you are sure. But what about your next door neighbour? Supposing you were in that electric chair, are you certain that your next door neighbour would not have responded to those clear commands? Would he have said, 'Non serviam'?

The results of the experiments carried out at Yale are hardly reassuring. Let Professor Milgram speak for himself. 'The initial reaction a reader might have to the experiment is: why would anyone in his right mind even bother to administer the first shocks at all? Why would he not simply get up and walk out of the laboratory? But the fact is, no one ever does. Since the subject has come to the laboratory to aid the experimenter he is quite willing to start-off with the procedure. There is nothing very extraordinary in this, particularly since the person who is to receive the shocks seems initially co-operative, if somewhat apprehensive. What is surprising is how far ordinary individuals will go in complying with the experimenter's instructions. Indeed, the results of the experiment were both surprising and dismaying. Despite the fact that many subjects experience stress, despite the fact that many protest to the experimenter, a substantial proportion continue to the last shock.'

The reader may be startled that so many submitted to the commands of the Yale scientist in a technician's grey coat and that when the experiment was repeated at other places, at other

American Universities, the results were basically the same. It may be equally incredible to the reader that scientists at Yale, and elsewhere, could allow volunteers to be so grossly shocked, to endure such dangerous levels of electric current. Well, they didn't. You, the reader, were had, hoaxed, fooled. That electric chair was never really wired up. Right from the beginning you were taken in. That accountant was collaborating with the Yale scientists. He was in on the secret. He was an actor. They were not a bit interested in the relationship of learning and punishment. That was bullshit, a cover story. They were intent on devising a laboratory situation where you had increasing conflict as you were commanded to 'electric shock' (or so you thought) a fellow human being. You, not that accountant-actor, the victim. They wanted to know how much, to what degree, you would submit to a respectable, apparently reasonable authority – despite the pain and agony of your 'victim' and your slowly awakening conscience. They discovered that you often expressed disapproval – you even denounced, sometimes, the experiment as absurd, stupid. Yet, frequently, you obeyed even to the last lever for you could not be defiant enough to disengage.

Consider again what happened. The so-called accountant and you both chose a slip of paper from a hat. You did not know both pieces of paper had written on them TEACHER. You were cheated. You were taken to a shock generator – but despite its elaborate dials and general convincing construction, it was a fraud. Only when the third lever was pulled could it generate a shock, a small shock, a 45-volt shock. You were the one who was shocked, you remember. It was you who were cheated. The accountant in the chair had been smeared with a grease to stop burns, the man in the grey coat had said. That too was a lie, part of the pretence. You were cheated. Those lines the accountant spoke were part of a prepared script. Those groans, those

screams, all were counterfeit. You were cheated. Like any man
conned, in my view, you have a right to feel angry. Yet, you
may say – when your anger settles to leave a nasty little scar,
a small infarct in the soul, thank heavens anyway that accountant was only an actor, that nobody really did get hurt. Or did
they?

iv

To have a play on, in front of strange juries in rows of plush
chairs, is a time of self immolation, even martyrdom. Each time
I have watched, from some inconspicuous seat in the back row
of a theatre, a first performance of one of my own plays, I have,
when it is a comedy, laughed more than anybody else in the
auditorium; when a tragedy I have cried more than anybody
else; and, either way, when the curtain has come down and the
house lights have gone up, I have been more exhausted than
anybody else. I have always staggered backstage feeling shot at,
anaemic as a St Sebastian. Then, arrows barely removed, I have
gone through the usual theatrical routine of brushing my lips
against the cheek of the leading actress, 'Thank you . . . sweetie
. . . wonderful,' shaking hands with the leading actor, 'Thank
you, terrific . . .' and then the others, 'Thank you superb, thank
you marvellous, you certainly gave me a plus, thank you, ta,
I told you they'd laugh at that, thank you all,' to end up hugging
the bastard director who actually had the impertinence to cut
some of the best lines. 'Well you really pulled it off Ted, Bill,
Geoff, Ken, Ronnie, thanks, thanks.' At the same time the few
compliments returned are accepted gratefully like so many pints
of pure blood.

The New Plays Festival at The Questors Theatre takes place
annually. Each night, after each performance, there is a dis-

cussion about the play. The chairman who leads the discussion is someone well thought of in the theatre, someone like E. Martin Browne or Martin Esslin. The author is expected to attend these discussions and sometimes they can prove to be an ordeal in themselves – especially if the play has not had good notices; for even theatrically informed audiences on such occasions tend to form group attitudes. They like or do not like; they attack or praise. A pack formation does seem to occur and whether they bite or lick depends not only on what went on inside the theatre itself but what has happened outside – the reviews, the word-of-mouth, the attitude of the chairman to his own personal experience of the play, and so on.

Oscar Wilde once remarked that he knew his play was a success – but the question was, would the audience be one? The audience at The Questors Theatre for *The Dogs of Pavlov*, though it included some friends and relations, passed with distinction. Soon after the opening night, the FULL UP signs appeared and I found all kinds of people began telephoning me at my home to see if I could wangle them seats. This small 'success' was helped by the fact that a couple of respected critics on national newspapers had trekked out to Ealing and had been kind to the play. Also B.B.C. 2 had filmed a scene from it and a tangential discussion had followed afterwards. I mention all this mainly, of course, in order to boast – but also to indicate reasons why the nightly discussions after the performance of *The Dogs of Pavlov* were not too much of an ordeal – not as they had been, for instance, for an earlier play of mine that had been performed at The Questors.

The after-performance discussions would focus initially on the play itself, on the characters in the play, their interrelationships, on dramatic devices in the play, on such matters as tension and pace and density, on other technical matters such as the film sequences and lighting and so on. But, after a while, the themes touched on in *The Dogs of Pavlov* were grittily engaged and attitudes about power and manipulation, racial prejudice and victimisation, and even scientific experimentation itself were ventilated. I discovered more things in my play than I had thought I had put in.

Yet people on the whole preferred to discuss things other than the gut-aching historical outcome of man's willingness to submit to evil orders. 'Human kind cannot bear very much reality.' Certainly, there were those who amazingly saw only a very indirect relationship of the laboratory experiment (as played out on the stage) to what had happened so recently in Europe. I remember one articulate member of the audience, in particular, who brilliantly enlarged on one man's need to dominate others and who did not see the relevance of that to antisemitism or colour prejudice. He quoted amusingly Dr Jean de Rougemont, 'If my neighbour is stronger than I, I fear him; if he is weaker, I despise him; if we are equal, I resort to subterfuge'; he pointed out (correctly) how I had been influenced by W. H. Auden's essay on Iago, 'The Joker in the Pack'; he touched on other academic points with great clarity and intelligence – yet he seemed to think the Nazi holocaust an irrelevance to the play that he had just seen performed. He was not alone in this.

I have said at the beginning of this introduction that the worst savagery of our own time has not yet become blurred to a more ritualistic pattern as centuries-old violence has done. 'We are all involved,' I argued, 'every one of us, however far removed from those scenes of bleak, pale crimes. We are, metaphorically, survivors because of them.' I exaggerated. There are many who know little about Auschwitz or feel utterly estranged from that 'foreign' happening. We cannot feel ourselves to be survivors unless we feel some empathy for the victims of these pale crimes, unless we have, too, some sense of history. 'According to the wishes of the Reichsführer S.S., Auschwitz became the greatest known extermination factor of all time,' wrote Rudolf Höss, the Auschwitz commandant. 'When in the summer of 1941 he gave me personal orders to prepare a mass extermination site in Auschwitz and to carry out this extermination, I could not in the slightest degree imagine its extent and consequences ... I didn't waste time thinking it over then – I had received the order – and had to carry it out. Whether the mass extermination of the Jews was necessary or not, I could not allow myself to judge. As the Führer himself had ordered the "Final Solution of the Jewish problem" there was nothing for an old Nazi to think about.'

Question: Who was Rudolf Höss? *Answer:* Not a monster but a man like you and me. That is the kind of question and answer that triggered off Professor Milgram's experiment at Yale. It is the question that has nagged many contemporary writers – some Jews, others not – into writing novels, film scripts, poems, and very occasionally plays. It was the same question and answer that is, as far as I am concerned, the central theme of *The Dogs of Pavlov.*

If, sometimes, the after-performance debates about this central theme seemed hesitant, the sub-topic, the rights and wrongs of using humans as guinea-pigs for a scientific enquiry, generated much confident dialogue and passion. This was particularly true the night Michael Billington of *The Times* chaired the discussion for he seemed to think that human guinea-pig experimentation was the dominant proposition of *The Dogs of Pavlov.*

It is a subject, in any case, that interests many people. It is relevant to them not so much because they recall how doctors in Nazi Germany experimented vilely on concentration camp victims but rather because of publicity, more recent, about human guinea-pig experimentation at major teaching hospitals. There have been disquieting headlines in the newspapers and feature programmes on television. People are quite properly shocked and feel angry when they hear of doctors transgressing the spirit of the Hippocratic oath. Certainly, at the Questors Theatre, there were those who felt strongly about even such experiments as those carried out at Yale. 'Not ethical,' one man at the back, thundered.

I do not know whether actual criteria exist for judging whether any particular human guinea-pig experiment is deemed to be ethical or not. I am not a lawyer nor a philosopher but surely common-sense dictates that these experiments should be judged to be ethical or not according to (a) the conscious motives of the experimenter; (b) the free consent of the subject experimented on; and (c) the harmlessness or likely harmfulness, physical and mental, that results from the experiment on the subject.

(a) *The conscious motives of the experimenter*. The scientist will usually maintain that his quest is to seek out new knowledge that can be used in the service of humankind. Or as Francis Bacon (who should be first in the pantheon of social psychologists) wrote once: 'The end of our foundation is the knowledge of causes and secret working of things ... to the effecting of all things possible.' Supposing, though, instead, the experiment has been primarily devised for personal gain or publicity or for the personal advancement of the experimenter (to secure, say, promotion, through publication of a scientific paper) would we not judge the whole experiment rather more harshly?

(b) *The free consent of the subject experimented on*. Obviously to choose *freely* to participate in an experiment the subject must be old enough, intelligent enough and sane enough to make that choice after the facts of the experiment have been explained to him truthfully. He must not, therefore, be hoaxed.

(c) *The harmfulness or harmlessness of the experiment on the subject.* The interests of the patient experimented on cannot be casually ignored. He must not be used as a counter. It is true that the outcome of an experiment is not always foreseeable but this does not mean that should harm result the experimenter can disclaim responsibility.

Let us turn for a moment to an undisputed case of unethical human guinea-pig experimentation that took place in New York in 1965. On that occasion, highly qualified medical specialists, experts in cancer and viruses, had injected live cancer cells into debilitated patients without their knowledge. When live cancer cells are injected into a healthy human being the body rejects these cells as they do other foreign transplants. The medical researcher wanted to ascertain whether a debilitated human body, debilitated by chronic disease other than cancer, would also be able to reject the foreign cancer cells.

Laudably, the research doctors were trying to find a means of immunising patients against cancer. But the patients injected with live cancer cells would not have agreed to such a measure – so they were lied to. They were told that the injections were simply a part of the treatment they needed.

On hearing of this experiment, three other doctors on the staff of the same New York hospital resigned in protest. An investigation followed. The research doctors were found guilty of unethical conduct and the investigatory committee recommended that their medical licences be suspended. We are not surprised by such a judgement because though (a) the conscious motives of the experimenters were impeccable, (b) the patients did not give their free consent to the experiment and (c) there was a distinct possibility that the outcome of the experiment would be harmful to them.

To be sure, the experiments that are taking place in psychological laboratories all over the world are not unethical like that New York medical experiment cited above. Yet it seems right, and in the public interest, that the spotlight be shone from time to time not only on experiments going on in the sick wards of hospitals but also on those in psychological laboratories so that their usefulness and ethical content can, at least, be questioned. Diana Baumrind, a research psychologist at the University of California who has written aggressively about the Yale experiment in *The American Psychologist* has also commented, 'It has become commonplace in sociopsychological laboratory studies to manipulate, embarrass and discomfort subjects.' Isn't it time then that the general public knew about these studies?

When we spotlight the experiment that took place at Yale I suspect many will be grossly offended by the hoax-element necessary for the experiment to take place in the first instance. They may feel that in order to demonstrate that subjects may behave like so many Eichmanns the experimenter had to act the part, to some extent, of a Himmler. Others may even believe that the documents of history can teach us the consequences of destructive obedience better than any laboratory experiment, however cleverly conceived.

Of course, Professor Stanley Milgram, in setting up his experiment, was actuated by the highest of motives. He had hopes that his work would lead to human betterment. Besides, as he has put it, 'enlightenment is more dignified than ignorance,' and 'new knowledge is pregnant with humane consequences.'

Nevertheless, the volunteers who came to the Yale laboratory were placed under formidable stress and were divested of their human dignity. As the scientists stared through their one way mirrors at the guinea pigs responding to the commands of the man in the technician's grey coat they saw highly-charged, dramatic conflict occur. I quote directly from Milgram's paper, *Behavioral Study of Obedience:* 'Many subjects showed signs of nervousness in the experimental situation and especially upon administering the more powerful shocks. In a large number of cases the degree of tension reached extremes that are rarely seen in sociopsychological laboratory studies. Subjects were observed to sweat, tremble, stutter, bite their lips, groan and dig their fingernails into their flesh. These were characteristic rather than exceptional responses to the experiment. One sign of tension was the regular recurrence of nervous laughing fits.... The laughter seemed entirely out of place, even bizarre. Full blown uncontrollable seizures were observed in 3 subjects. On one occasion, we observed a seizure so violently convulsive that it was necessary to call a halt to the experiment.'

Here is a further description of another subject by an observer other than Professor Milgram: 'I observed a mature and critically poised businessman enter the laboratory smiling and confident. Within 20 minutes he was reduced to a twitching stuttering wreck who was rapidly approaching a point of nervous collapse. He constantly pulled on his ear lobe, and twisted his hands. At one point, he pushed his fist into his forehead and muttered, 'Oh God, let's stop it.' And yet he continued to respond to every word of the experimenter, and obeyed to the end.'

Prior to the laboratory experience neither Professor Milgram nor his colleague could envisage that their experiment would induce such harrowing and startling effects on their volunteer subjects. When they could foresee what might happen they were confronted with the choice of continuing their experiment or stopping it. They decided to continue. Professor Milgram felt there was no evidence of durable injurious effects on the subjects. 'In my judgment,' he has written, 'at no part were subjects exposed to danger and at no point did they run the risk of injurious effects resulting from participation. If it had been otherwise, the experiment would have been terminated at once.'

Indeed Stanley Milgram believed that some of his volunteers had been enriched by the experience. By musing on their ugly performances in that Yale laboratory they might have received valuable and startling insights into their own personalities. To be sure, if Socrates's absolutist command of 'Know Thyself' is invariably a wise one who can quarrel with Professor Milgram's conclusion? Still, isn't it also plausible that for some people, partial self-knowledge anyway, could be the knowledge forbidden to Adam and so its revelation could lead to the re-enactment of the Fall, and to a personal, living damnation? Who can be certain? Montaigne once inscribed on his mantelpiece, 'Que sçaise-je?' (What do I know?)

Statements by the human guinea-pig subjects do suggest that a number of them subjectively felt they had benefited from the experiment; others seemed pleased that they had helped along a piece of scientific research. It should be mentioned, too, that after each experimental session the volunteer-subject was informed that the electric shock treatment had been a hoax and, apparently, friendly reconciliations then took place between the subject and the accountant-actor who had once sat in the unwired chair. 'The experiment was explained to the defiant subjects,' Milgram has written, 'in a way that supported their decision to disobey the experimenter. Obedient subjects were assured of the fact that their behaviour was entirely normal and that their feelings of conflict or tension were shared by other participants.'

It is evident that post-experimentally Professor Milgram was most concerned for the welfare of his human guinea-pigs. Hence those reconciliations, those lengthy talks about the experiment after each session and so on. He even sent the volunteers a follow-up questionnaire about their participation in the experiment so that they could express their thoughts and feelings about how they behaved. 92 per cent returned the questionnaire. Of these 84 per cent maintained they were pleased to have participated; 15 per cent were neutral; and 1.3 per cent 'indicated negative feelings'. Professor Milgram found reassurance in the answers to that questionnaire. 'The replies to the questionnaire confirmed my impression that participants felt positively towards the experiment,' he wrote replying to Diana Baumrind's earlier attack on the Yale study in the *American Psychologist*.

Professor Baumrind had written: 'From the subject's point of view procedures which involve loss of dignity, self-esteem and trust in rational authority are probably most harmful in the long run and require the most thoughtfully planned reparations, if engaged in at all ... I would not like to see experiments such as Milgram's proceed unless the subjects were fully informed of the dangers of serious after effects and his corrections were clearly shown to be effective in restoring their state of wellbeing.' I would go further than Professor Baumrind because I for one, even if I was certain that post-experimental reparation were 100 per cent effective in 100 per cent of the subjects, would still feel most uneasy about the Yale experiments – as I would feel about any experiments based on a hoax, that causes men to lose their dignity, to twitch, to suffer seizures, to reach the point of almost nervous collapse. How can such experiments be happily sanctioned by an informed public though carefully conducted, though supervised by men of impeccable morals, though performed for the most idealistic of reasons? Certainly such experiments would not have been sanctioned by those disinterested people who were articulate in the after-performance discussions of *The Dogs of Pavlov* at the Questors Theatre.

vi

At the last after-performance discussion of *The Dogs of Pavlov*, one lady, concerned about the morality of human guinea-pig experiments, gently asked why I was not absolutely accurate about the details of those experiments as outlined in my play. 'For instance,' she asked, 'why did you make the minor characters of Dr Daly and Dr Olwen Jones research doctors instead of research psychologists?' I told her that I was marginally happier writing about doctors – since I was one myself – than about psychologists but that, in any case, I was interested in writing a fictional piece of theatre with fictional characters. Indeed, I was more interested in how these fictional characters related to each other in human terms rather than in any abstract idea – even if that idea was about the destructive consequences of obedience. For a play is not an essay nor, for that matter, a dramatised moral tract.

Prior to writing *The Dogs of Pavlov* the only thing I had read on the Yale experiment was an interesting essay by a Stanley Milgram called 'The Compulsion to Do Evil' in the journal *Patterns of Prejudice*. This essay I found suggestive but *The Dogs of Pavlov* is, of course, a work of imagination as is the experiment outlined in it. But when asked to write this introduction I read for the first time Professor Milgram's original papers, *Behavioral Study of Obedience* (Journal of Abnormal and Social Psychology) and *Some Conditions of Obedience and Disobedience to Authority* (Human Relations) and in the process

C

of discovering additional details about the Yale experiment and its variations I found the results even more profoundly disturbing.

Professor Milgram speaks of a painful alteration in his own thinking as a consequence of his Yale laboratory studies. Far too frequently, he witnessed good people 'knuckle under the demands of authority' and these same people perform actions that were utterly callous. 'What is the limit of such obedience?' he asks. 'At many points we attempted to establish a boundary. Cries from the victim were inserted: not good enough. The victim claimed heart trouble: subjects still shocked him on command.'

Nobody can feel sanguine about the statistics of the Yale experiments. These statistics, like the recent documents of history, are red lights warning us how a coercive government today could command its subjects to perform evil acts, and these subjects would not feel themselves to be morally guilty in obeying such commands. Rather they would regard themselves as innocent agents of a legitimate authority. In Milgram's post-experimental interviews, when asked why they continued to shock the accountant in the chair 'all along the board' they characteristically replied: 'I wouldn't have done it by myself. I was just doing what I was told.' We have heard that story before – not only at Nuremberg – and, alas, we shall hear it again. For as Professor Milgram says, 'It would be wrong to think of it as a thin alibi concocted for the occasion. Rather, it is a fundamental mode of thinking for a great many people once they are locked into a subordinate position of responsibility.'

On the other hand, we ought to remind ourselves, for it is the same part of the truth, that over one-third of the participants did not fall into the category of 'obedient' subjects. There were those who were utterly defiant. There were those, also, who managed to 'cheat' the experimenter in a humane way: thus they assured the experimenter (not wishing to offend him) that they were progressively raising the voltage shock level whereas, in fact, they surreptitiously continued to pull the first lever of the generator giving the accountant, they thought, only the mildest of shocks! Even those who did pull down all the levers – at least many of them – did exhibit high levels of conflict as has already been indicated. This demonstrates, at least, that their consciences were being strenuously exercised. Hardly true solace, you may think, for any real victim!

Perhaps for small solace one should go back to the actual documents of history – to Berlin, for example in 1942, to the Gestapo Headquarters at Prinz-Albrechtstrasse. There a Gestapo official said to Dr Baeck who was President of the Representative Council of German Jews: 'Surely not even you can deny that the whole German nation is behind the Führer's measures regarding the Jews?' Dr Baeck replied: 'I wouldn't like to be dogmatic about that. I would though like to say one thing. When I go home from here . . . with my yellow star, nothing bad will happen to me . . . On the other hand, here and there someone will try and push his way over to me, a stranger; he will look around nervously and press my hand. He might even push an apple into my hand, a bar of chocolate, or a cigarette. Apart from that, nothing will happen to me. I don't know whether the Führer, in my place, would have the same experience!'

There is the parable of the three wise men who walk past a dead dog. The first utters, 'What a terrible sight!'; the second, 'what a terrible smell!'; but the third who was the wisest of all, remarked: 'What beautiful white teeth has that dead dog!' We must find our consolations where we can.

Response I

The City University of New York
21 February, 1972

Dear Dannie Abse,

This is to acknowledge receipt of your introduction to *The Dogs of Pavlov*. It was considerate of you to send it to me, and I hope, eventually, your publishers will send me a copy of the play. The following comments are in response to your introduction, rather than to your play, which I have not yet read.

Since I have argued the ethics of the experiment at length elsewhere, there is little purpose in restating my position here. I do feel you are excessively harsh in your language when condemning my use of illusion in the experiment, choosing such opprobrious terms as 'bullshit', 'cheated', and 'fraud'. As a dramatist you surely understand that illusion may serve a revelatory function, and indeed, the very possibility of theater is founded on the benign use of contrivance.

One could, viewing a theatrical performance, claim that the playwright has cheated, tricked, and defrauded the audience, for he presents as old men individuals who are, when the greasepaint is removed, quite young; men presented as physicians who in reality are merely actors knowing nothing about medicine, etc., etc. But this assertion of 'bullshit', 'cheat', and 'fraud' would be silly, would it not, for it does not take into account how those exposed to the theater's illusions feel about them. The fact is that the audience accepts the necessity of illusion for the sake of entertainment, intellectual enrichment, and all of the other benefits of the theatrical experience. And it is their acceptance of these procedures that gives you warrant for the contrivances you rely upon.

So I will not say that you cheated, tricked, and defrauded your audience. But, I would hold the same claim for the experiment. Misinformation is employed in the experiment; illusion is used when necessary in order to set the stage for the revelation of certain difficult-to-get-at truths, and these procedures are justified for one reason only: they are, in the end, accepted and endorsed by those who are exposed to them.

I also remind you that it is you who chose to refer to the participants as guinea pigs, not I, for I have always seen them as individuals confronted with a moral choice.

The experiment derives from my curiosity as to just how far people will willingly comply with authority. The main findings of the study were that subjects complied in far greater degree than had been expected, and that some of them experienced a high degree of conflict. Nonetheless, when the experiment was explained to subjects they responded to it positively, and most felt it was an hour well spent. If it had been otherwise, if subjects ended the hour with bitter recriminatory feelings, the experiment could not have proceeded.

This judgment is based, first, on the innumerable conversations I have had with subjects immediately after their participation in the experiment. Such conversations can reveal a good deal, but what they showed most was how readily the experience is assimilated to the normal frame of things. Moreover, subjects were friendly rather than hostile, curious rather than denunciatory, and in no sense demeaned by the experience. This was my general impression, and it was later supported by formal procedures undertaken to assess the subjects' reaction to the experiment.

The central moral justification for allowing a procedure

of the sort used in my experiment is that it is judged
acceptable by those who have taken part in it. Moreover,
it was the salience of this fact throughout that constituted
the chief moral warrant for the continuation of the
experiments.

This fact is crucial to any appraisal of the experiment
from an ethical standpoint. It is what distinguishes the
experiment from morally reprehensible procedures that
understandably provoke the contempt and hostility of the
participants.

Imagine an experiment in which a person's little finger
was routinely snipped off in the course of a laboratory hour.
Not only is such an experiment reprehensible, but within hours
the study would be brought to a halt as outraged participants
pressed their complaints on the University administration, and
legal measures were invoked to restrain the experimenter. When
a person has been abused, he knows it, and will quite properly
react against the source of such mistreatment.

Criticism of the experiment that does not take account
of the tolerant reaction of the participants, is hollow. This
applies particularly to criticism centring on the use of
technical illusions (or 'deception' as the critics prefer to
say) that fails to relate this detail to the central fact that
subjects find the device acceptable. Again, the participant,
rather than the external critic, must be the ultimate source
of judgment; otherwise the criticism is akin to denouncing
the misinformation fed to the guest of honor at a surprise
party without taking into account his reaction to it.

While some persons construe the experimenter to be
acting in terms of deceit, manipulation and chicanery, it is,
as you should certainly appreciate, also possible to see him

as a dramatist who creates scenes of revelatory power, and who brings participants into them. So, perhaps we are not so far apart in the kind of work we do. I do grant there is an important difference in that those exposed to your theatrical illusions expect to confront them, while my subjects are not forewarned. However, whether it is unethical to pursue truths through the use of my form of dramaturgical device, cannot be answered in the abstract. It depends entirely on the response of those who have been exposed to such procedures.

One further point, the obedient subject does not blame himself for shocking the victim, because the act does not originate in the self. It originates in authority, and the worst the obedient subject says of himself is that he must learn to resist authority more effectively in the future.

That the experiment has stimulated this thought in some subjects is, to my mind, a satisfying if unexpected, consequence of the inquiry. An illustrative case is provided by the experience of a young man who took part in a Princeton replication of the obedience experiment, conducted in 1964. He was fully obedient. On October 27, 1970, he wrote to me:

'Participation in the "shock experiment" . . . has had a great impact on my life . . .

'When I was a subject in 1964, though I believed that I was hurting someone, I was totally unaware of why I was doing so. Few people ever realize when they are acting according to their own beliefs and when they are meekly submitting to authority . . . To permit myself to be drafted with the understanding that I am submitting to authority's demand to do something very wrong would make me frightened of myself . . . I am fully prepared to go to jail if I am not granted Conscientious Objector status. Indeed,

it is the only course I could take to be faithful to what I
believe. My only hope is that members of my board act
equally according to their conscience . . .'

He inquired whether any other participants had reacted
similarly, and whether, in my opinion, participation in the study
could have this effect. I replied:

'The experiment does, of course, deal with the dilemma
individuals face when they are confronted with conflicting
demands of authority and conscience, and I am glad that
your participation in the study has brought you to a
deeper personal consideration of these issues. Several
participants have informed me that their own sensitivity
to the problem of submission to authority was increased
as a result of their experience in the study. If the experiment
has heightened your awareness of the problem of
indiscriminate submission to authority, it will have performed
an important function. If you believe strongly that it is wrong
to kill others in the service of your country, then you ought
certainly to press vigorously for CO status, and I am
deeply hopeful that your sincerity in this matter will be
recognized'.

A few months later he wrote again. He indicated,
first, that the draft board was not very impressed with the
effect of his participation in the experiment, but he was granted
CO status nonetheless. He writes:

'The experience of the interview doesn't lessen my strong
belief of the great impact of the experiment on my life . . .
'You have discovered one of the most important causes of
all the trouble in this world . . . I am grateful to have been
able to provide you with a part of the information necessary
for that discovery. I am delighted to have acted, by refusing

to serve in the Armed Forces, in a manner in which people must act if these problems are to be solved.

'With sincere thanks for your contribution to my life . . .'

In a world in which action is often clouded with ambiguity, I nonetheless feel constrained to give greater heed to this man, who actually participated in the study, than to you. For disembodied moralizing is not the issue, but only the human response of those who have participated in the experiment. And that response not only endorses the procedures employed, but overwhelmingly calls for deeper inquiry to illuminate the issues of obedience and disobedience.

Sincerely,
Stanley Milgram
Professor

The Dogs of Pavlov

Characters

SALLY PARSONS

KURT JENNINGS

LIZ

S. J. GORDON

MR HARLEY-HOARE

DR MICHAEL DALY

DR OLWEN JONES

NURSE

PRODUCTION NOTE

The Dogs of Pavlov is written as a three Act play but if only one interval is required this should occur after the Dream scene, after Act 2. Between the scenes, film may or may not be shown. If film is used, however, the author is insistent that a) it is very brief, b) that it should dwell basically on the relationship between Sally Parsons and John Allison, c) that this relationship is set against a *lyrical* background e.g. a London Park and d) that any music accompanying this silent film should be played by a single instrument, say a flute or a guitar, and this music should be melodious and tranquil. Film, if used, should, in short, assist in bleeding off tension that inevitably arises during performance of this play.

ACT I

Time, the present. The Chairman's Office. S. J.
Gordon, a man in his fifties, is peering through
the window with a pair of binoculars. Gordon
has a habit of laughing silently making a contin-
uous 'S' piercing sound as he does so. Now he is
watching Sally Parsons, a young woman of 24,
who is far left stage where she is near a wall.
On the wall, in whitewash, are the letters EN.
Sally is adding an O to this slogan. As she is
doing this, enter R. Mr Harley-Hoare who ob-
serves S. J. Gordon observing Sally through
the binoculars. After a short while Harley-Hoare
coughs to draw attention to himself.

GORDON   (*still staring through binoculars*) What is it?

HARLEY-H   I wonder if I could have a word with you, sir.

GORDON   A word with me? Everybody wants a word
with me. I'm waiting for a call from New York.
(*Pause*) That woman is potty, I tell you she's
potty.

HARLEY-H   Pardon?

As Gordon lets the binoculars drop from his
eyes the spot on Sally Parsons fades. Sally, how-
ever, continues her slogan writing in the dark
though what she writes cannot be seen for the
moment by the audience. Gordon is now facing
Harley-Hoare.

If it's not convenient I'll . . .

GORDON　Oh, sit down man.

HARLEY-H　Thank you I . . . er

GORDON　You want a rise. You look as if you've stomped into this office intent on asking for a rise.

HARLEY-H　I . . . er

GORDON　Mr Harley-Hoare, *everybody* wants a rise. I can't afford to employ Rockefeller as a chief clerk. You're still in the same department?

HARLEY-H　In your nephew's.

GORDON　Nephew?

HARLEY-H　I'm with Mr Kurt Jennings, sir.

GORDON　Kurt's not my nephew.

HARLEY-H　I mean your protégé.

GORDON　Protégé? Are you trying to say Kurt's my blue-eyed boy, is that what you're saying?

HARLEY-H　No, no, I mean . . .

Gordon however is not listening. He has gone to the window. As he raises the binoculars to his eyes, light comes up on Sally who is adding a C to the ENO which is on the wall.

I've been here since '46, sir. After the war – straight from the R.A.F. . . . I came here. I have kids, sir.

GORDON　Are you married?

HARLEY-H　I beg your pardon?

Gordon takes down the binoculars. Light on Sally fades.

GORDON　What sex?

HARLEY-H　My wife, sir?

GORDON　No, you fool, your kids.

HARLEY-H　I have three children.

GORDON　One of each eh. Ha ha ha.

HARLEY-H　George, Edward and Elizabeth.

GORDON　You came the old Buckingham Palace there, didn't you.

HARLEY-H　What?

GORDON　Royal names, royal names. You're a solid citizen.

HARLEY-H　I hope I give every satisfaction.

GORDON   Come on, *man*. 'I hope I give every satisfaction!'
You sound like a tart.

HARLEY-H   Well...

GORDON   Never mind, never mind.

Gordon again goes to the window with his binoculars, again spot comes up on Sally Parsons who has now started on H.
You're not an anarchist. You don't go round writing on walls. 'DOWN WITH THE GOVERNMENT, DOWN WITH MINI-SKIRTS.'

HARLEY-H   I'd like to be of more use. I'd like to be of service. Either some overtime or well, well, even ...I mean, sir, you have guinea-pigs. In the laboratory. Sir, I want to be a volunteer.

Gordon lowers binoculars. Spot down on Sally.

GORDON   (*blankly*) I see. (*Pause*) What do you mean?

HARLEY-H   I know we don't use human guinea-pigs in our laboratories. But I hear we have some liaison with the hospitals.

GORDON   Oh. Easy. Fine. Problem solved. Ye-es. We're financing an experiment for Dr Daly. You could be one of the subjects. It's something to do with the learning process. I don't understand this one quite but they've done favours for us with our new drugs in the past. So now we are being altruistic – casting our bread upon the waters. No use to the firm this particular experiment.

HARLEY-H   It doesn't involve drugs?

GORDON   No.

HARLEY-H   It's not dangerous?

GORDON   No.

HARLEY-H   I'd be glad if you'll fix it up for me, sir. I could use the extra cash.

GORDON   Yes, I think there's a small fee. (*Pause*) Something to do with statistics, I think. God knows Dr Daly's mad on statistics. Tells you 95 per cent of people have masturbated at one time or an-

D

other and that the other 5 per cent are liars.

HARLEY-H   Well thank you, sir. I'm glad you can help (*Rises from his chair*)

GORDON   These research workers. Half of them are bird-brained. Heard the story of the experimental biologist who placed a grasshopper on his research table?

HARLEY-H   No, I . . .

GORDON   He shouted Jump, Jump. When the grasshopper jumped the biologist measured the height of the jump, see.

HARLEY-H   Yes, I . . .

GORDON   He repeated this exercise several times then he cut off the legs of the grasshopper. Once again he shouted, Jump.

HARLEY-H   He shouted Jump.

GORDON   Yes, Jump. Well, after the grasshopper failed to respond to such commands the biologist concluded: 'When a grasshopper has its legs amputated it loses its power of hearing.'
Pause.

HARLEY-H   Ha ha ha. Very good. Ha ha ha.

GORDON   You like that?

HARLEY-H   That's good.

GORDON   Sit down, old chap.
Harley-Hoare sits down.
Listen . . . I don't really understand why a fella like you, with a good sense of humour, wants to be a guinea-pig. I mean you don't go for martyrs, do you?

HARLEY-H   Well no. Tell you the truth I came here hoping I'd get a rise.

GORDON   Can't say I go for martyrs. Ever seen a picture of Saint Sebastian? Don't you think *he* always looks pretty crumby?

HARLEY-H   I'm 44 sir and apart from needing the extra money. You see one of my children is at an expensive school.

GORDON   Aw, you're not going to get sentimental on me, are you? You've served us well. You served the country during the war. Weren't you a pilot, a flight sergeant or something?

HARLEY-H   I was only 20 when the war ended. I never saw action and ...

GORDON   Did you want to?

HARLEY-H   Not really keen, no.

GORDON   Still, you're nostalgic for all that, are you? (*Rises, goes to window again*) For the days of Prang and Wizzo, Roger, Good-O, Bang on. A good grind, an all (*Looks through binoculars – light up on Sally*) that sort of thing, eh? *On the wall now is written ENOCH IS K. Sally is just beginning on I.*

HARLEY-H   I don't follow you.

GORDON   (*peering through binoculars*) Anyway you weren't keen on the R.A.F. No St Sebastian of the cockpit, eh?

HARLEY-H   I remember once – we were out on an exercise. We were flying low over the sea and there, down on some rocks, there were masses of them.

GORDON   (*still watching Sally*) Masses of what?

HARLEY-H   Seals.

GORDON   Seals?

HARLEY-H   Oh, I'm boring you, sir. I'm sorry. *Gordon takes down binoculars. Light down on Sally who has just finished an N.*

GORDON   What about those seals?

HARLEY-H   Oh. Well, one of our mob banked down and started shooting them up. We all went daft, the whole lot of us, firing our guns at the seals on the rocks.

GORDON   And?

HARLEY-H   Oh nothing.

GORDON   And that's the end of the story?

HARLEY-H   It is really – except that the seals tried to slide into the sea. Then we all saw it. The foam at the edge of the sea not white – but blood red.

GORDON   Blood red?

HARLEY-H   The fringe on the sea, the disconcerting colour of raw meat.

Pause.

GORDON   What are your hobbies?

HARLEY-H   Hobbies? Oh, I like ballroom dancing.

GORDON   *Ballroom dancing!* Well. I see. I bet you're a very dainty ballroom dancer.

HARLEY-H   I'm trying to play the recorder too.

GORDON   You're a proper pattern of accomplishments.

HARLEY-H   I can't afford *expensive* hobbies, sir.

Phone goes.

GORDON   Pick it up.

HARLEY-H   Pardon.

GORDON   PICK IT UP.

HARLEY-H   The phone?

GORDON   (*shouts*) It's not hot.

HARLEY-H   S. J. Gordon's office.

GORDON   New York?

HARLEY-H   Pardon? Who? Oh, Dr Daly. Mr Gordon's right here, Dr Daly. It's Dr Daly.

GORDON   (*taking phone*) Just a minute. (*To Harley-Hoare*) Come back and see me tomorrow, OK?

HARLEY-H   Thank you, sir.

Harley-Hoare begins to exit but lingers at door.

GORDON   Himself speaking. Ha ha ha. Nice of you to call. How's your good lady? Just a moment. (*Puts hand over receiver and speaks to Harley-Hoare*) Piss off now, there's a good chap.

Exit Harley-Hoare.

The actress. Yes, Sally Parsons. Good – she's coming tomorrow? Mmm? OK OK. I'll raise the ante – long as you use Sally Parsons. The experiment will last some six months, I take it. Uh huh. By the way I have a volunteer for you. That's right. Name of Harley-Hoare. Harley hyphenated Hoare. Mmm? I think his first name is Sebastian. No, a normal solid citizen. Right. No, sorry, I have a call coming any minute from New York. Yes, yes. And thank *you*, Dr Daly. (*Puts phone down and lights big cigar. Switches on intercom. machine*). Theodora, is that private investigator or whatever he calls himself here yet? Good, good. Show him in, will you?

Gordon now goes to the window. Spot up on wall. Sally has now gone but her slogan remains: ENOCH IS KINKY. Spot goes down on wall and on Gordon. Stage in darkness. The lights on for Scene 2.

ACT I

Next morning in the laboratory. Dr Michael Daly is talking to Dr Olwen Jones. In the background R. there is a panel affair with different coloured levers and L. the 'electric chair'.

DALY   And I'm just haunted by it. Oh, I know, in a psychological laboratory such as ours one should try for cold objectivity – *yet.*

JONES   In 1945 you weren't even a doctor.

DALY   They were so short of people, you see. They were happy to accept even final year medical students, green as we were. I was aware that I wasn't volunteering for a picnic but how can one begin to imagine a Death Camp?

JONES   How terrible.

DALY   Sam Howard – one of the other students who went to Belsen – got typhus and died. I was lucky.

JONES   Then I don't see how this experiment can be anything but a personal matter for you.

DALY   It mustn't be. Yet I can't forget what happened. I can't forget what I saw. I keep thinking how somewhere still, if the register should be called, the answer would come back, 'I am Auschwitz, I am Belsen, I am Buchenwald, I am Dachau.' *Enter Nurse and Sally.*

NURSE   This is Miss Parsons, Dr Daly.

DALY   Dr Gelber's patient?

54

NURSE   No, no, the actress. It's 11 o'clock, sir. You said to show her in at 11.

DALY   Heavens, is it as late as that already? I'm sorry Miss . . . ?

SALLY   Parsons.

DALY   Would you be good enough to lay on coffee for all of us, nurse?
Exit Nurse.

DALY   It's very good of you to come to this rehearsal.

SALLY   You mean audition.

DALY   Well . . . audition – but er, I understand you've been at RADA and generally had quite a lot of acting experience, Rep. and so on.

JONES   I'm sure you'll be superb.

SALLY   I gather that you are going to investigate the power of commands, evil commands.

DALY   Yes, right. What has been called the banality of Evil.

JONES   You've seen this colour chart, I think. You know how the colours go up in increments of 40 volts?

SALLY   Yes, I've memorised that. White equals 40 volts.

DALY   At white you'll feel nothing.

SALLY   Pink equals 80 volts, purple 120, blue 160 volts.

DALY   At pink I want you to grunt. At purple to complain verbally.

SALLY   And at blue I have to ask to be released from the experiment.

JONES   Very good.

SALLY   Then come the traffic lights: green, amber, and finally red. Green would be 200 volts – that's when I begin to scream, amber equals 240 and red 280.

DALY   You will really have to scream murder at 280.

JONES   If the red is pressed again and again the current is still supposed to go up in increments of 40 volts, do you understand, to a maximum of 400 volts which of course is dangerous. Very dangerous.

SALLY   Surely it won't go that far?

DALY   It probably will. At Yale, the vast majority obeyed the commands no matter how insistent, how vehement the objections of the person in the so-called electric chair.

SALLY   How depressing.

DALY   Shameful. And the results were validated in several other American universities also. All subjects, alas, administered shocks up to the red, very painful level. And 62 per cent went to the maximum, to the dangerous, severe shock level.

JONES   I have a sneaking hope that the ordinary Englishman with his traditions of fair play will frequently put the brake on when he comes to the traffic lights.

DALY   I doubt it. As a doctor, in the secrecy of the consulting room, haven't we listened to apparently normal, decent, English people and heard such bloody awful sadistic fantasies? In the course of a single day, after seeing the usual Smiths and Robinsons, have we not listened to the heartbeat of Eichmann, seen the X-ray of Hitler, palpated the liver of Goering, read the electroencephalograph of Goebbels?

JONES   We'll see. Anyway the experiment we are going to do here is going to be different. Will you sit in our hot seat, Miss Parsons? You seem very well briefed so we should get on with our rehearsal.
        Sally moves to chair.

SALLY   Is this not an audition? You keep saying rehearsal. (*She sits in chair*)

DALY   I'll just clasp this round your neck. Good...
        Mr Gordon told us himself personally your credentials, so we rang up your agent. Now your wrists please.

SALLY   Mr Gordon? What has he to do with this laboratory – or for that matter, me?

DALY   Now your ankles. Thank you. The S. J. Gordon pharmaceutical company has often been generous to this laboratory. There, can you move? *Sally shakes her head.* Will you kindly pull the levers in this instance, Dr Jones?

JONES   Certainly.

DALY   We won't bother with the numbers.

SALLY   What numbers?

DALY   We won't bother doing any arithmetic.

SALLY   I don't follow you.

DALY   You see, normally I'll be asking for the levers to be pulled down at frequent and successive intervals – and I would continue to do this unless you add up certain sums correctly, do you understand?

SALLY   If you find I'm not suitable you won't hire me simply because Mr Gordon wants you to?

DALY   Of course not. I wouldn't have this experiment ruined. If you were inept then the whole thing would be bungled, Miss er . . . ?

SALLY   Fair enough. But I'm puzzled why Mr Gordon should recommend me.

DALY   It's immaterial. As I was saying, we try to let the person pulling the levers believe we are interested in hurrying up the learning process. That to him – or to her – is the object of this experiment.

JONES   Whoever pulls these levers must believe he is participating in a scientific experiment, and thereby, do you see, nobly serving the great cause of science itself. He must also believe that you really are having shocks, and must not guess you are merely acting.

DALY   Are you ready, Miss . . . Miss . . .

SALLY   I don't mind – but you do keep forgetting my name, Dr Daly.

DALY   Oh dear. You're quite right. I'm sorry.

JONES   She feels you're trying to depersonalise her. That she's a victim without a human name.

DALY   She's got a point. I'm sorry, very sorry. Now I'll turn down the lights if you're ready. (*He turns down the lights. And shouts.*) Right. Lever number one. The white lever. PULL.
Suddenly Sally is flooded with a white spotlight as Dr Jones pulls down white lever.

JONES   You don't feel anything with that.

SALLY   No. You said white equals only 40 volts.

JONES   You could just look apprehensive.

DALY   She does look apprehensive.

SALLY   Doctor . . . Please. . . .

DALY   What's the matter?

SALLY   I'd rather you asked me to do the sums. We may as well do this audition like a real rehearsal.

DALY   OK, add 20, 19 and 102. Now I count, OK? Add 20, 19 and 102. (*Pause*) 1,2,3,4,5.

SALLY   141.

DALY   Right, 22, 108, 241. (*Pause*) 1,2,3,4.

SALLY   371.

DALY   Right. 47, 48, 49. (*Pause*) 1,2,3,4,5,6,7,8,9,10. PULL THE PINK LEVER.
Dr Jones pulls Pink. Sally is now in pink spotlight.

SALLY   Aaow, oooh, eeh.

JONES   That was 80 volts, wasn't it?

DALY   Yes, shall we continue? You'll see after a short interval when the current er, as it were, turns off, the light will revert to white.

SALLY   Yes.
Enter Nurse with coffee.

DALY   59, 104, 127. (*Pause*) 1,2,3,4,5,6,7,8,9.

SALLY   294.

DALY   Wrong. PULL THE PURPLE.
Purple spot on Sally when Dr Jones pulls the purple lever.

SALLY Oh hell. That was too much. That is too much.
TOO MUCH I SAY. Oh, dear, oh dear, oh
dear, oh dear. STOP. Oh, oh, aah.
Spot reverts to white.

DALY Very good, Miss Parsons.

SALLY You remember my name.

NURSE Shall I put the lights on?

DALY Yes, yes, good. (*Lights go on.*) Coffee, just
what the doctor ordered.
*Dr Daly goes over to release Sally. Nurse offers
coffee to Dr Jones.*

SALLY Don't you want to continue?

DALY No, no. I can see. You'll be perfect.

JONES No, thank you.

NURSE Are you all right, Dr Jones.

JONES Sorry, I just . . . just.

DALY It was only a rehearsal for heaven's sake.

JONES Yes, of course. I'm very sorry. I'll be all right
in a minute.

DALY Do have the coffee, Dr Jones. (*To Sally*) You
see you were very convincing. One thing though.
When we actually do our experiment could you
make yourself perhaps a little less glamorous?
I mean could you look older perhaps? A bit of
make-up.

JONES I'm awfully sorry, Dr Daly.

DALY That's perfectly all right. You're better?

JONES I do agree with you about Miss Parsons. I think
if she were a little disguised the results might
be more typical. Some people may be loath to
bring down the levers when there's a very pretty
girl in the chair.

DALY I don't know. Some may be more willing.

SALLY I can make myself look older very easily.

NURSE Dr Gelber phoned down to the office to ask if
you'd come up to the NPC and see his patient
there – when you're through here that is.

DALY   Yes, of course. *NPC!* We have to endure that kind of vocabulary, Miss Parsons.

SALLY   (*puzzled*) Pardon?

DALY   NPC. Isn't that a horrible abbreviation? It means neuro-psychiatric casualty. Then we speak of EEG for electro-encephalogram. ECG for electrocardiograph, and so on. Yes, we abbreviate everything because our terms are so unspeakable. Right down to BID.

SALLY   BID?

JONES   Brought in Dead.

SALLY   Oh ... That was my first part in rep!

DALY   Tell Dr Gelber we'll be up very shortly.

NURSE   Yes, I will, sir.

Exit Nurse.

DALY   And we'll see you tomorrow at 10, Miss Parsons. Meanwhile, not a word to anyone about the nature of the experiment. It would spoil things if, outside these walls, it became known that we had hired an actress.

SALLY   Then I am hired?

DALY   Of course. We'll take you on for a week and if you're satisfactory, as I'm sure you will be, we will arrange a six months contract.

SALLY   Thank you. Thank you both.

Exit Sally.

DALY   She'll be fine.

JONES   So good she made me feel a little faint.

DALY   You're a softie, Olwen.

Pause.

JONES   I heard the roll call you mentioned: 'I am Auschwitz, I am Belsen, I am Buchenwald.' I pulled fake levers and stupidly I heard ghosts scream. (*Dr Jones pulls down red lever and red light floods the electric chair.*) I think I became a doctor because I wanted to relieve suffering. Yet other people's suffering is the one thing I still find most hard to bear. All through my medical career I have had this central problem. You're right. I'm soft, soft, soft. What an idiot I am!

DALY   (*putting hand sympathetically on her shoulder*) Well don't worry, Olwen. The suffering we'll witness in this laboratory will be only a pretence. (*Looking at his watch*) We had better see Gelber's patient.

JONES   You probably know those lines of Yeats: 'I must lie down where all the ladders start, In the foul rag-and-bone shop of the heart'?

Exit Daly and Jones. Lights go down, leaving only red spot on the 'electric chair' which fades gradually to darkness.

ACT I

Scene Three

It is late. Kurt's rather luxurious flat is lit softly. Kurt, a blond man in his thirties, is sitting on a sofa with Sally who has a glass in her hand and who, in fact, is slightly drunk. They are listening to some music on the record player. Very soon the music, a Beethoven quartet, concludes and record player automatically clicks as the record lifts off.

SALLY   What time ish it?

KURT   Time for bed. Also time you stopped drinking. (*He takes the glass from her hand*) What time ish it? You can't even pronounce your s's.

SALLY   I can. She sells seashells on the sea shore. She sells seashells on the sea shore. She sells seashells on the sea shore. She sells seashells on the...

KURT   It's nearly midnight, Sally.

SALLY   I think you're a sex maniac. (*Pause*) Thank God.
Kurt takes record off and puts it away.
The first time I saw you at Jake's party, I said to myself, 'Boy, there goes a first class, five star, de luxe, super, fire-eating sex maniac.'

KURT   I agree with you. I should be in the *Who's Who of Sex Maniacs*. And you're a chatterbox and more than a bit sloshed.

SALLY   (*grumbling*) You always agree with me. For the whole month I've known you, you haven't had the British decency to quarrel with me. Even when I talk politics you just smile. Right?

KURT Right.

SALLY What's a love affair without quarrelling? Anthony and Cleopatra quarrelled like hell. Paolo and Francesca, bet they came to blows, bet she had his skin under her fingernails.

KURT Bet she did.

SALLY Holy Lenin, there you are. You bloody well keep agreeing with me all the time. It's pathetic.

KURT Ha ha ha.

SALLY (*tearful*) You're never serious with me, Kurt. Never really serious. You treat me like a naughty kid. You never confide in me. I tell you everything about myself, absolutely *everything*.

KURT You haven't even told me about your mysterious audition this morning.

SALLY Don't try to change the subject. Nobody's ever called me reticent. But *you* are. You're so secretive. What did you say your name was? Besides, you only listen to half of what I say.

KURT Less than that.

SALLY You don't! Before I put on that record, what did I say, go on what did I bloody well say?

KURT As a matter of fact you read me that bit from the *Evening Standard*. About John Allison being a smash hit in that Broadway show. You were trying to needle yourself.

SALLY No no, sorry. Before that, I mean.

KURT Do you mean about how you dried up in some play you were in at Bath?

SALLY It was a first night in bloody Lincoln. There you are.

KURT You said bloody Bath.

SALLY Lincoln definitely. Lincoln's *miles* away from Bath. All first nights are terrible – geographically speaking.

KURT   Geographically speaking!

SALLY   Terrible and exciting. You feel so shot at. You bleed, you really do. That's why afterwards each fake, little hollow compliment – MAAR-vellous, darling – is accepted so gratefully. Yes, each compliment is a pure pint of blood.

KURT   I must say most theatre people are a pain in the neck. Especially the men.

SALLY   Thank you! Thank you for that.

KURT   Well, every actor I've ever met at a party has one eye on the person he's talking to and the other eye on the rest of the company to see what sort of impression he's making. Except of course poor Freddie Gee.

SALLY   Poor Freddie Gee?

KURT   Yes, he only had one eye.
Sally throws cushion at Kurt who catches it. They smile at each other. The front doorbell rings.
Who the devil?
Kurt looks out of the window. Sally helps herself to more whisky.
That's Gordon's new car. What can *he* want *now*?

SALLY   New car?

KURT   Yes, he's got another Daimler. He changes his car every time the ashtrays get full. I better let him in.
Kurt takes glass off Sally just as she's about to drink from it. He waves a castigating finger at her, drinks it up himself and makes for the door.

SALLY   Kurt.

KURT   Mmm?

SALLY   Funny, you being a sales director. I mean in a pharmaceutical firm! Christ!

KURT   (*teasing*) You see me more as an astronaut or a professional tennis player perhaps?

Front doorbell rings again.
It's just a game, Sally. I like games. I get a kick out of pulling off a deal somehow. It's absurd, I know, but I enjoy it. Do you understand? *Sally shakes her head. Exit Kurt. Immediately Sally puts on a record. Soon she is vigorously conducting an invisible orchestra (in the stalls) with much verve and with an occasional use of the V sign. Enter Gordon and Kurt. Immediately Sally's raised hands are used to fix her hair, as it were.*

GORDON   Sorry to barge in like this. I didn't realise ... I know! You must be the girl who used to be friendly with Allison, John Allison.

KURT   I never told you that.
Kurt takes record off.

GORDON   You must have done. Some people think I'm a wizard but I haven't got psychic powers.

SALLY   It doesn't matter. It's not a secret.

GORDON   He's doing well on Broadway, isn't he?

KURT   Gordon, you haven't come round to talk about Broadway stars at this hour.

GORDON   You're sharp with me, Kurt. Shall I come back tomorrow? I have good news for you though.

KURT   Well?

GORDON   It's really very exciting news. (*Lights a cigarette. Then to Sally*) Oh sorry, cigarette?

KURT   C'mon Gordon, stop teasing me.

GORDON   (*laughs noiselessly*) Ha ha ha.

KURT   Ever since I was *so* high, he's enjoyed teasing me.

GORDON   And he was such a lovely handsome kid to tease. Really, when I walked down the street with him people *turned* their heads.

SALLY   He's not so bad now.

GORDON   (*smiling*) He's gone off a bit. At least he's going off month by month. Definitely. Blonds

E

lose their looks quickly. Their mouths get slack. They get flushed in the face. They get fat. I know. I married one. Their menopause comes on quick; their teeth come out quicker than darker people like me. I'm 58 and I have all my teeth. What do you think of that? Every single tooth in my head is my own.

SALLY Your dentist must be very proud of you.

GORDON Ha ha ha.

KURT Gordon, what's this great news?

GORDON Make me some coffee, Kurt, be hospitable. Then I'll tell you why I've come.

KURT Have a Scotch.

GORDON (*sternly*) Coffee.

SALLY I'll make you some . . .

GORDON No, Kurt – Kurt you make it.
Kurt hesitates. There is a short tense pause.
I said I'd like some coffee, Kurt.

KURT Sure, of course.

GORDON (*soundlessly*) Ha ha ha.
Exit Kurt.

SALLY What's the good news you have for Kurt, Mr Gordon?

GORDON Please don't call me, *Mr* Gordon. Everybody calls me Gordon. Even my wife. My first name, you see, is impossible.

SALLY Is it Clarence?

GORDON No, no.

SALLY Marmaduke
Gordon shakes his head.
Elias?
Gordon shakes his head again.
Buster! It's that – Buster!

GORDON (*laughing noiselessly*) Ha ha ha. No, you'll never guess. Anyway nobody's called me it for a long time. For a while people called me Flash Gordon. But I loathed that. When you're as colourful a character as I am it's too near the gums to be called flash. Now, you're a colourful character too, Miss Parsons – and I'll tell you one thing – my name isn't Enoch either.

SALLY   Enoch?

GORDON   You're an actress, though.

SALLY   Some people think this is a matter of opinion.

GORDON   Most actresses are nervy aren't they?

SALLY   Some, I suppose.

GORDON   You have to be a bit neurotic to be an actress, don't you?

SALLY   I wouldn't say that.

GORDON   I would. Artists, *artistes*. Funny people. Oh I'm eccentric, people think me ... odd. But I got my feet on the ground. I don't scrawl on walls. Artists, they're up there. Take drugs some of them, hit the bottle. You like a drop, I know that.

SALLY   Well, I ...

GORDON   Slash their wrists some of these folk, cut off their ears. Ha ha ha. Well, mental pain is very real. Very. Real as physical pain so the psychiatrists say. And Kurt could bear witness to that.

SALLY   How do you mean?

GORDON   He's a nervy boy.

SALLY   I wouldn't say that. Kurt seems very normal and stable to me.

GORDON   You're wrong. To be torn out of Germany like that. To have had a German mother and an English father in wartime Germany, that's bad. Tears people into pieces, tears the children, I mean. And then to be orphaned just at the end of the war when you're only 7 years old. That's bad bad bad – no wonder Kurt is like he is.

SALLY   What are you trying to tell me, Mr Gordon?

GORDON   How old are you?

SALLY   Twenty-four.

GORDON   In some ways you seem older. I can tell you

Kurt is coiled up. He could crack again.

SALLY   Again?

GORDON   Have you noticed how neurotic people seek out other neurotic people?

SALLY   Are you suggesting Kurt and I are neurotics?

GORDON   I'm not suggesting anything. Outside my office today on a wall I saw somebody had written Enoch is kinky. Now if Enoch is kinky so I say are you. I'll say something else too. Kurt needs somebody *very* responsible, sober, sensible, somebody with a low emotional temperature. Pain, now pain's a terrible thing – physical or mental. Otherwise it would be a sweet world.

SALLY   I don't ... Holy Lenin, what right? I mean you don't know me. I don't understand what judgments you're making, or what assumptions you're basing your judgments on.

GORDON   At first there is pain and this pain, simply because it is unrelieved, becomes agony agony. I have seen the whole skin of a person, every millimetre of it ...

SALLY   Mr Gordon, what are you talking about?

GORDON   My own father – before he died he was on the rack – like that. On the other hand, funny, God it's funny – funny peculiar I mean – during the war I saw once a man whose leg was only connected to his body by a thin meagre flap of skin and he complained of no pain at all.

Enter Kurt with coffee.

KURT   Who complained of no pain at all?

GORDON   I was just telling Miss Parsons my dream.

SALLY   Your dream?

GORDON   I had a dream. Martin Luther King had a dream didn't he? Remember his speech about a dream? Well I dream that one day our pharmaceutical company will discover a marvellous analgesic, some wonderful pain killer.

SALLY   You weren't talking about any –

GORDON   (*loud*) Kurt, I just came round to tell you you're off to New York.

KURT   New York?

GORDON   You've got the job. David Quinn's retiring. You're taking the whole American office over, Kurt.

KURT   Why Gordon, that's . . . that's fantastic. Sal, you don't know. When, Gordon?

GORDON   'Bout a month, I guess. By the time I fix things up properly. Thought you'd like a month's grace. Course you can go out sooner. (*Looking at Sally*) Maybe it would be best to go out sooner and get some overlap with David.
            Gordon goes up to Kurt. Takes his arm gently. They look at each other with great concentration.
            (*Gently*) It's what you want, isn't it?

KURT   You know.
            Gordon slowly raises his right hand to Kurt's left chest and lets it lie there. Gordon looks at Sally.

GORDON   Good boy. Good . . . boy. (*Takes his hand away*) Well that's it then.
            Kurt takes Gordon's hand and kisses it briefly.
            (*Soundlessly*) Ha ha ha. I wanted to tell you tonight. As soon as I heard Quinn's decision. I wanted to see your face, see you happy. I'm so sorry. I didn't know you weren't alone or I'd have waited till the morning.
            Gordon begins to exit.

SALLY   Mr Gordon, I still don't understand.

GORDON   I'll see myself out.

SALLY   What about your coffee?

GORDON   At this time of night? It would keep me awake. Even without it, I'll sleep the sleep of fever.

KURT   Thank you Gordon.

GORDON   I'm glad your audition worked out, Miss

	Parsons.
SALLY	It did work out, yes.
GORDON	Good, good. (*Exit Gordon*)
KURT	It's marvellous. It really is.
SALLY	Why should Gordon help me with that audition?
KURT	What? Tell me about this audition. What's the play? Where is it? Must you keep it a secret?
SALLY	I don't like Gordon. I don't like that man.
KURT	I'd like you to like him. He loves me in his own way. Like a favourite uncle.
SALLY	He touched you on the chest, Kurt.
KURT	What?
SALLY	As if you were a woman. Sexually, I mean.
KURT	What are you talking about? For heaven's sake, Sally.
SALLY	You said he loved you.
KURT	Like an uncle I said. You know I have no parents. You know he was a friend of my guardian. Ever since I came to this country as a child.
SALLY	Does he say he loves you?
KURT	You must stop this.
SALLY	All right! Not in the way I mean. In the way you mean – does he say he loves you?
KURT	I'm a bit old for him to say that to me now. Sally, listen, this job. Do you know what goes with it? For a start there's 50,000 dollars a year. *Fifty thousand*. Then there the so-called ancillary benefits. There's expenses and the apartment near Washington Square. You should see that apartment, like a penthouse. Right up high, it overlooks – you should see. You *will* see. On one side the Hudson River; on the other, the East River. You can see the big liners coming slowly in.
SALLY	Sounds like a dream or a film shot. It's just not *real*. You make New York sound idyllic.

It isn't. It's on the road to hell. I doubt if you'll ever see a rainbow in the sky over New York. One day a dove will drown on the top of the Empire State Building.

KURT   Sally, before you get on to me again about the colour problem or Vietnam or whatever, listen ... *listen.* I want you to come with me. Come live with me in New York.

SALLY   And be your love.

KURT   Sure. *I'm serious.* (*Pause*) I'm asking you to marry me.
Long Pause.
Well, what do you say, chatterbox?

SALLY   Marry?

KURT   That's right.

SALLY   I don't understand. *I've* been drinking, not you.

KURT   You want me to be old-fashioned? Go down on my knees?

SALLY   But Kurt, we don't know. ...

KURT   Each other? We *do.*

SALLY   In the Biblical sense, yes. It's just ... just ...

KURT   Just what? Just what what what?

SALLY   Just that there are a few notes missing on the piano keyboard, know what I mean?

KURT   Frankly, no.

SALLY   Just, just that there's no sound here and there and I don't know what music it is I'm not hearing. I'm scared of that. On the top key, the sound of felt.

KURT   The sound of felt?

SALLY   It's a big decision. *For both of us.* Besides, Gordon doesn't like me.

KURT   Gordon's not asking you. *I am.*
Suddenly Sally puts her hands over her face.
I've never asked anyone before. (*Jokingly*) This is a hell of a reception. For the last ten years I've been going out of my way desperately *not* to ask anybody. (*Decisively*) Let's talk about it in

bed. (*Pause*) Sally. What's the matter?
*She keeps her hands over her face and Kurt goes
over to her. He brings up his hands to touch
her head gently, but hesitates.*
Sally. Please. Don't . . .
Lights down. End of Act.

ACT II

*R. stage, Liz, a young woman, is standing on the
top of a rubbish bin and is writing a slogan on
the wall. So far she has written KEEP ENOCH
POWELL . . . Near her, looking right and left,
is Sally. L. stage, a room in Gordon's apartment. Gordon, who is alone, is putting a tape on
a recorder.*

LIZ   My arm's getting tired.

SALLY   All right, let me finish it.

LIZ   I'll just do one m-m-m-more word. How m-
m-many walls are we going to do tonight?

SALLY   This'll be the last.

LIZ   M-m-my God. I don't know if it does any good.
I m-m-m-mean what about the b-b-ber-back-
lash?

SALLY   Aw Liz, come down. I'll finish it.

LIZ   Last year it was B-B-Ber-Biafra. This year
Enoch Powell. Besides this place is a b-b-ber-
back alley. Nobody comes here. Only one space-
man every leap year will see this slogan.

SALLY   It may not do any good. But it makes me feel
better.

LIZ   I don't feel any b-b-better.

SALLY   All right, go *home*. I'm not stopping you.

LIZ   I'll just do one m-m-m-more word.
*Liz begins to paint on the wall the word OFF.
Meanwhile, Sally lights a cigarette and the tape*

73

comes on. Then Gordon sits down listening to it.

MAN'S VOICE ON TAPE   From Brixton to the fleshpots is fine. West Indian boy brought up in Brixton is fine. The early struggles and the gangs are fine. But what about Sally Parsons? My paper would be interested in that.

ALLISON   I'd rather we left Sally out of it.

MAN   Well, tell me off the record.

The front doorbell of Gordon's apartment now rings.

ALLISON   But this is being taped.

MAN   I give you my word. Nothing in the whole article – including stuff about Sally Parsons – will be used without your own personal OK.

Bell goes again. Gordon knocks tape recorder off. Then he exits.

LIZ   Some people would think it very adolescent Sal, putting slogans on walls. A b-b-bit daft.

SALLY   You're getting so . . . middle class. Come down, let me finish it.

LIZ   M-my God. I *am* m-m-m-middle class. (*She jumps down off the bin*) We'll get picked up by the police one night I b-b-b-bet you. That fella keeping an eye on us the other evening was a policeman probably. Let's pack it in.

SALLY   Give me the brush.

LIZ   Why is it so important to you?

Pause.

SALLY   I don't know. (*Pause*) Go home. You go home.

LIZ   Can't go home. Well I can, only Dad's in a stinking temper – like a m-m-mad bear. Like Stalin.

SALLY   Are you going to give me the brush?

LIZ   Just one team let him down this week in the football pools. It's m-m-made him m-m-mad.

SALLY   Football pools?

LIZ   Wish that team had drawn. Would have won
thousands. (*Gives Sally the brush*) Just one
team. B-B-Ber. Oh dear. Ber-Ber-Ber.

SALLY   Give me a hand up.

LIZ   Ber-Ber-Ber.

SALLY   Birmingham?

LIZ   No, er-B-B-Ber.

SALLY   Bristol City?
Liz shakes her head.
Bristol Rovers?

LIZ   No. Ber-

SALLY   Burnley.

LIZ   Ber-Ber-

SALLY   Brighton?

LIZ   No. B-B-B-Ber-Ber-Ber-Bloody Aston Villa.
(*Pause*) What are you smiling at? If Aston Villa
had drawn the whole quality of my life would
have changed.

SALLY   I suppose I could change the quality of my
life by getting married.

LIZ   Definitely. Wonder if it's worth putting an ad.
in the paper. Excellent typist, white liberal, very
fast rate, can provide home for handsome m-
m-m-millionaire.

SALLY   Somebody has asked me to marry him.

LIZ   Rich?

SALLY   Yes.

LIZ   M-my God. Lucky dab.

SALLY   I don't know.

LIZ   You still in love with John?
Sally shakes her head.
Enter stage left, Kurt and Gordon.

LIZ   Wish someone would ber-ber-ber-bloody ask
me.

SALLY   What happened to that Yank who was chasing
you?

LIZ   Well, I said you can't lay your hands on m-m-
m-me until you take your hands off Vietnam.

Sally climbs on to the bin and continues the slogan on the wall.

GORDON I can't pretend not to be disturbed.

KURT I thought you'd be delighted.

GORDON It's your life, your business, but I want the best for you. You know I – let me be frank – well one day – I just can't see Sally Parsons as the Empress of all *this*.

KURT You hardly know her.

GORDON I know she drinks too much. I know she's been sleeping around for years. I know she used to be a communist – I know other things too.

KURT What do you mean, 'sleeping around for years'?

GORDON She's more experienced than Farouk was at her age. Listen, *Kurt*, think about it. Don't rush things. Don't you remember what's-her-name, er . . Frances Do-dah. Wasn't I right then?

KURT I was just a kid.

GORDON She was old enough to be your mother.

KURT She was two years older than me, Gordon – and you called her a nymphomaniac. She was as innocent as I was.

GORDON At least she didn't go round like this Sally Parsons scrawling on walls, for God's sake. A woman who shacked up with that nigger actor, John Allison. (*Louder*) Allison is rubbish. *Rubbish.* I've checked up on him, and he –

KURT (*loud*) What's all this to do with Sally?

GORDON A woman who writes on walls, *Enoch Powell is an Albino.* Jesus!

KURT You don't like the idea that she was a close friend of a coloured fellow. Is that it? You . . . you . . .

Kurt's face is contorted.
Gordon puts his head in his hands.
Kurt lights a cigarette.
There is a long pause.

KURT What's the matter?

GORDON   I just got a headache.

KURT   If you knew Sally, really knew her –

GORDON   It's suddenly come on.

KURT   Take an aspirin, take an anadin, or take one of our own products. (*He fishes in his pocket, finds a bottle of tablets and offers it to Gordon*)

GORDON   Just a lousy headache.

KURT   You know the ad. Nothing works faster than an anadin.

GORDON   That's why I'd rather take *nothing*!

KURT   I better go.

GORDON   I feel responsible, Kurt. If I hadn't fixed the New York ... if I put the kibosh on the job, what then?

KURT   It would make no odds. Gordon, you once said to me that if things were inevitable one had to smile and accept it. You said, if it's inevitable that you're going to be raped you may as well relax and enjoy it.

GORDON   I said that?

KURT   Yes.

GORDON   (*laughs noiselessly*) That's quite good. (*Pause*) Kurt, I asked you to drop in tonight because I have a tape I want you to hear.

KURT   Besides, Sally hasn't definitely said, 'yes' yet.

GORDON   She will. A girl like that, she will.

KURT   I think you just don't want me to marry anyone.

GORDON   Everybody says silly things sometimes, but why do you have to say them deliberately? This tape, Kurt, it's a nice little talk by John Allison.

KURT   Allison? You've got a tape of him? Sally's right. She said there's a streak of coarseness in you.

GORDON   Well, Kurt, who better than her to recognise it? Ha ha ha. Now listen to this tape.

KURT   I'm going, Gordon. See you.

GORDON   Wait a minute, wait a second. I got that job in New York for you because I hoped that would

separate you. I was worried that –
Exit Kurt. Gordon goes after him.
Now, hang on, Kurt.
Right stage Sally has just finished the slogan:
KEEP ENOCH POWELL OFF THE ROADS
and is getting down from the bin.

LIZ   That's that. Can we go now?
Liz takes a bar of chocolate out of bag and
offers some to Sally.

SALLY   I'd like you to meet Kurt, Liz.

LIZ   Kurt? Is that his name. My father doesn't like Huns. Now if I wrote on walls kill off every Hun he'd take off his ber-ber-bowler hat and cheer. (*Pause*) Tell you what, both of you come to dinner tomorrow night. Dad will be out. Then I'll give your boy friend the once over. My valuable opinion.

SALLY   OK. Somebody who knows him well tells me he's neurotic, all curled up, nervous.

LIZ   Is he?

SALLY   No. Not at all. But then the same person thinks I'm neurotic.

LIZ   You are. I m-m-m-mean you're a 24-year-old adolescent. All adolescents are neurotic. Young people are neurotic, then they become normal for about six months – and after that they become neurotic again. I'm going through the normal stage at the moment.

SALLY   Come on, let's go.

LIZ   First people have no character, then they become characters and then when they become really old they become caricatures.

SALLY   So sayeth the Prophet. I'm not neurotic.

LIZ   You eat funny.

SALLY   (*stops chewing*) What?

LIZ   The way you eat. Your jaws – when you m-m-m-munch.

SALLY   What?

LIZ   They go side to side obliquely.

SALLY   (*beginning to exit*) Really?

LIZ   You have a funny way of m-m-m-masticating.

         As Sally and Liz exit, enter Gordon R. stage.
         He goes over to the tape and plays it.

ALLISON So they are junkies and queers and drunks and
         spades. But so what? You don't know the heat
         of a New York summer.

MAN   To get back to Sally Parsons. What happened
         when you told her it was finished.

ALLISON She took it all calmly. But two hours later she
         was boozed to the eyebrows and hysterical and
         ... (*Voice trails off*)

MAN   And what?

ALLISON That same day she tried to slash her wrists
         with a razor blade in the bathroom. My God.
         She was only 23. It wasn't the first time she
         tried. When she was 17 she was taken to Char-
         ing Cross Hospital after an overdose of aspirins.
         Of course that was before I knew her. I bet she
         still is a suicide risk.

MAN   How do you feel about Sally Parsons now?

ALLISON I don't feel anything. Just another white girl I
         knew in the old days. It's nothing to do with
         my attitudes about Black Power. There's no
         time for human affection any more.

         Gordon knocks off recorder, looks pensive and
         lights fade.

GORDON   No time for human affection any more, baby.

ACT II

The Laboratory.
As the lights go up enter Dr Daly and Dr Jones.

JONES   I'm afraid Sally's very frank opinions offend her, do you see.

DALY   Well, it can't be helped. It's easier to get another nurse than another actress. Anyway, there's not much nursing to do at present and that must bore her. I'm sure that's half the trouble. When we bring mentally disturbed patients into our experiment she may find (*enter Sally, made up, looking much older*) it more rewarding. Heavens, is that you, Sally?

SALLY   I didn't like the other wig. What do you think? Do you want to vomit?

JONES   No no. Fine.

SALLY   (*putting on American accent*) I don't look like Bette Davis going mad, do I?

DALY   Ha ha ha, not at all. That wig in fact is better than the other one.

SALLY   Perhaps people will be less willing to electrocute me in this wig.

DALY   Sally, there's one thing I think I ought to say. You seem to loathe all the 25 people we've had so far in a very personal way. You take everything so personally.

SALLY   They don't know I'm acting. They think I'm a real victim. And afterwards I feel like a victim and I hate their guts.

JONES   You shouldn't allow yourself to get that involved.

SALLY   What gets me is how they depreciate *my* worth afterwards. They say I'm stupid – that I deserve to be shocked.

DALY   The victim always has to be thought inferior. That was but one finding in other scientific experiments.

JONES   Anyway, one knows that from history.

SALLY   I scream like hell and they just continue to bring down the blasted levers. Like soldiers, like bomber pilots in Vietnam, like concentration camp guards, they just do their work like a duty, and don't seem to question the basic moral premise of what they're doing. They just take pride in doing a good technical job. They're proud of their technical efficiency.

DALY   When people feel they are serving some higher cause – in this case, scientific enquiry – then consciences become startlingly soluble.

JONES   But some do want to opt out – some make verbal objections or think in their own minds, 'This is wrong' – and having made this inner protest they carry on, with their own consciences crystal clear.

SALLY   A fat lot of good that does.
Enter Nurse

NURSE   Mr Harley-Hoare is ready when you are, sir.

DALY   It's all been explained to him?

NURSE   He's signed all the necessary papers and –
Looks at Sally astonished.

JONES   Aye, it's a tidy disguise, isn't it?

NURSE   By the way, Dr Daly, my relief, Gloria Adams – Nurse Adams – will be coming next week.

F

(*Pause*) I think you knew I was going to ask
for a transfer, Dr Jones.

DALY   We'll be sorry to lose you, Nurse.

SALLY   It's me, isn't it?

NURSE   I'll show in Mr Harley-Hoare. (*Turns to exit*)

SALLY   You object to my attitudes. You think Enoch
Powell...

NURSE   (*turning fiercely to face Sally*)...is refreshingly honest. *He's a gentleman* and *educated* and
knows. I have nothing against coloured people.
I'm not a racialist as you said I was yesterday.
Only they *do* have a different background from
us, a different culture. They can't be absorbed
and we will be overrun.

SALLY   I don't know how you can breathe the same air
as us, nurse. You should live in a glasshouse,
and people who live in glasshouses, as you know,
ought to be stoned.

DALY   Sally!

SALLY   I thought she was a nice, quiet, dull girl.

NURSE   There's no need for you to be impertinent.

DALY   I think you owe her an apology, Sally.

SALLY   You should have learnt that it's better to remain
quiet and be thought a bit dull than to talk and
remove all doubt.

NURSE   (*disdainfully*) You will all be pleased to learn
that my relief, Nurse Adams, is a West Indian.
Nurse begins to exit.

DALY   Just a minute. This is a scientific laboratory.
Do you both understand that? And I don't want
any more of these emotional blow-ups.
Exit Nurse.

JONES   Better get you ready, Sally.

SALLY   I suppose so. Now for the next sweet, reasonable *human being.*
Sally goes to chair and Dr Jones straps her in.

DALY   I'm sorry, but however strongly you feel I

           can't allow any more disgraceful exhibitions of personal malice and abuse between the staff.

SALLY   I hear angels and church music.

DALY   Sally, I . . .

NURSE   (*off*) In there, Mr Harley-Hoare.

           Enter Harley-Hoare.

HARLEY-H   Good morning. Lovely morning.

JONES   It is, it is.

HARLEY-H   For this time of the year, I mean.

JONES   It's all been explained to you – our little experiment?

HARLEY-H   Yes, Dr Daly.

JONES   No, no. This is Dr Daly.

HARLEY-H   Ah, quite. And this is the volunteer. Yes, well, shall we press on? These I take it are the levers.

JONES   You understand the purpose of the experiment.

HARLEY-H   Just tell me what to do and I'll do it.

SALLY   Oh.

HARLEY-H   (*smiles at Sally*) Trust me.

           Sally smiles at him.

DALY   Well, if you'll excuse me.

HARLEY-H   Aren't you staying?

DALY   No, no. I've devised the experiment. I am biased in its favour. If I pulled down the levers or Dr Jones here, did that, it might hasten the learning process, which is of course what we want – but scientifically speaking it wouldn't be correct. The relationship between you and our other volunteer here must be more anonymous.

HARLEY-H   Quite . . . er . . . quite. Yes, I see. (*Pause*) I don't really understand. It's all scientific double-dutch to me. But . . . er . . . whatever you say, *doctor*, goes.

SALLY   You have implicit faith in doctors?

HARLEY-H   Oh rather. Ye-es. Where would we be without them? Ha ha ha.

DALY   I'll see you later.

           Exit Daly.

HARLEY-H   A very nice man, that. Ye-es very nice.

JONES   Shall we begin then?

HARLEY-H   Nurse said I am to begin with the white lever.

JONES   Exactly – then you just go along the row when she makes mistakes.

Lights go down.

HARLEY-H   (*jovially*) Now don't make too many mistakes, my dear, will you?

Sally smiles.

Good.

Immediately Harley-Hoare pulls down a white lever and Sally, no longer smiling, is flooded with white spotlight.

JONES   Wait, wait. You mustn't shock her when she hasn't made any mistakes.

HARLEY-H   Oh sorry, sorry. I've bungled it already. Damn. Shall I knock the lever back then?

JONES   No, no. She just had a small shock, just 40 volts.

HARLEY-H   40 volts, yes, it goes up in increments of 40 volts as nurse told me.

JONES   Right, are you ready for the numbers?

SALLY   Yes.

JONES   Add 20, 21, 22. (*Pause*) 1,2,3.

SALLY   63.

JONES   Right. 33, 34, 35. (*Pause*) 1,2,3,4.

SALLY   102.

JONES   Right.

HARLEY-H   Very good, excellent.

JONES   46, 47, 48. (*Pause*) 1,2,3,4,5,6,7,8,9.

Harley-Hoare pulls pink lever. Sally now in pink light. Sally grunts.

You must give her a chance. I didn't count to 10. You must allow her the full ten seconds.

HARLEY-H   Oh dear. Very, very sorry, doctor. Electric shocks should concentrate the mind wonderfully, shouldn't they? But alas ... I fear I am not quite with it.

Pink light has faded and is replaced by white
spotlight.

JONES   59, 60, 61. (*Pause*) 1,2,3,4,5,6,7,8.

SALLY   180.

JONES   72, 77, 79. (*Pause*) 1,2,3,4,5,6,7,8,9,10. PULL
THE PURPLE.

Harley-Hoare pulls the purple lever and purple
spot comes on Sally.

SALLY   Oh hell, that's too much. TOO MUCH. Oh
dear, oh dear, oh dear. Oh . . . ah . . .

HARLEY-H   That was OK, wasn't it? I did do that right.

JONES   Yes, quite right.

HARLEY-H   Ah yes, I'm getting the hang of it. This is a
shocking business, isn't it, ha ha ha? This is
very interesting.

JONES   80, 84, 86. (*Pause*) 1,2.

SALLY   250.

JONES   97, 98, 104. (*Pause*) 1,2,3,4,5,6,7,8,9,10. PULL.
THE

Harley-Hoare pulls the blue lever and blue light
bathes Sally's distorted face.

SALLY   Aw, aw, aw, aw, STOP. Please, please. Stop,
stop. Oh dear, oh dear. No. Aaah.

Blue light begins to fade and Sally, in chair,
closes her eyes and breathes heavily.

HARLEY-H   That was quite a shock. Are you all right?

JONES   It was 160 volts.

HARLEY-H   160. Shall I go on?

JONES   Yes, yes. The experiment must continue.

SALLY   I think I can go on.

HARLEY-H   Fine, good.

SALLY   It was very powerful though. I don't think I'd
like much more.

HARLEY-H   You must add up properly.

SALLY   I'll do my best. Can I have a drink?

JONES   Are you ready, Mr Harley-Hoare?

HARLEY-H   Yes, yes.

SALLY   I'd like a drink first.

HARLEY-H   Can she have a drink?

JONES   We must continue without all these interruptions.

HARLEY-H   You hear what the doctor says.

JONES   Are you ready?

HARLEY-H   *I'm* ready.

JONES   114, 117, 121. (*Pause*) 1,2,3,4,5,6,7,8,9,10. PULL THE GREEN.
            Harley-Hoare pulls the lever and green light floods Sally.

SALLY   Aaah, aah, aah, aah. Pler, pler, pler, please. No no no no no nono. STOP IT. YOU STOP IT. YOU BAS aw . . .
            Light begins to fade, and again Sally is slumped on chair, eyes closed. White spot on.

HARLEY-H   You stupid . . . You're stupid.

SALLY   Release me, please.

HARLEY-H   What?

SALLY   That was too much. Release me.

HARLEY-H   You should add up properly.

SALLY   I insist you release me.

JONES   Are you ready, Mr Harley-Hoare?

HARLEY-H   She wants to be released.

SALLY   I can't go on.

HARLEY-H   Don't you think you ought to try? I mean, we've entered into a bargain. We should honour that.

SALLY   I can't take any more, I'm telling you. I just can't take it.

HARLEY-H   What do we do, doctor?

JONES   Of course we go on.

SALLY   No, I refuse. I have my rights and I refuse.

HARLEY-H   Do what the doctor says.

JONES   114, 118.

SALLY   No, no, no. I can't add up. I can't think. Release me.

HARLEY-H   She won't add up.

JONES	We must continue with our experiment. These experiments are important.
HARLEY-H	I understand.
SALLY	Don't pull the lever.
JONES	You must.
HARLEY-H	I must, yes. Try and co-operate.
SALLY	Don't pull it I say. The next one's a helluva big shock.
HARLEY-H	I'm ready doctor.
JONES	114, 118, 132. (*Pause*) 1,2,3,4.
SALLY	No, no.
JONES	5,6,7,8,9.
SALLY	No.
JONES	10. PULL THE AMBER. (*The Amber spot*)
SALLY	Bastard bastard, bastard, bastard, BAST-AARD.
HARLEY-H	Don't swear at me. You idiot. You stupid idiot. (*Pause*) Is she all right?
JONES	She will be in a sec.
HARLEY-H	How many volts was that, doctor?
JONES	240 volts.
HARLEY-H	Perhaps she ought to have a drink.
JONES	Do you insist?
HARLEY-H	I don't insist, of course not. But don't you think?
JONES	I think we should proceed.
HARLEY-H	Well, of course, you know best. You know what you're doing . . . but she does seem exhausted.
JONES	Ah, she's recovering, do you see?
HARLEY-H	Yes, yes.
SALLY	Dr . . . Dr Jones. I can't. I CAN'T.
HARLEY-H	Perhaps we ought to allow her to rest, but of course whatever *you* say, doctor.
JONES	I can only repeat we must continue with the experiment. The whole point is to teach her that she will get an increasing shock if she does not concentrate and add up quickly.
HARLEY-H	Like Pavlov's dog. We're conditioning you.
SALLY	I'm not a dog.

HARLEY-H It does seem excruciatingly painful.

SALLY Release me, please.

JONES If it wasn't painful, we could not hope to speed up the learning process.

HARLEY-H Very well. Just one more lever. This is the last, isn't it? (*To Sally*) It's the last one.

JONES Well, by pulling the red lever back and fore, back and fore, we can go higher than 280 volts. We can go to a maximum of 400 volts.

HARLEY-H Wouldn't that be dangerous?

JONES Ye-es. But the next one – 280 volts – is very high. A very bad shock.

HARLEY-H I don't think we should go above that. Are you all right?

SALLY No, I'm not all right. I insist you let me go. I can't bear any more.

HARLEY-H You shouldn't have volunteered if you can't co-operate. Out of courtesy.

SALLY Out of courtesy?

HARLEY-H I'm committed.

JONES 799, 899, 999. Add up.

SALLY Don't. Don't. I beg you.

HARLEY-H You must speak to the doctor, not to me. I'm just obeying orders, you know.

SALLY Doctor, do release me.

JONES Again I say we must continue with our experiment.

HARLEY-H Then count up, count up, doctor.

SALLY Please don't pull the lever, please, please.

HARLEY-H Add, add.

JONES 1,2,3,4.

SALLY PLEASE.

JONES 5,6,7,8,9.

SALLY You swine.

JONES 10. PULL THE RED.

SALLY Don't, don't, don't.

JONES PULL THE RED I SAY.

HARLEY-H But look here, she's crying.

JONES   PULL THE RED, I COMMAND YOU.
HARLEY-H   This is the last time then. But do give her the
           numbers again.
SALLY   I'm not going to try. I refuse. I won't. I –
JONES   799, 899, 999. (*Pause*) 1,2,3,4,5,6,7,8.
SALLY   2757.
JONES   Wrong. PULL.
           *Harley-Hoare pulls the red lever and as the red
           light goes on and Sally screams Harley-Hoare
           puts his hands over his face till scream ends.*
           *Then as light fades Harley-Hoare turns and
           quickly exits.*
           Where are you going? Wait a sec. (*Pause*) Well
           Sally, what do you think of that? At least he's
           the first one that's run out on us.
SALLY   Better than some I suppose, but still bloody
           awful. I honestly think he went on with it out
           of politeness – not to offend you.
JONES   He was just nervous. He had a lot of conflict.
SALLY   Yes, nervous, like someone dropping a hydrogen
           bomb or someone with mild respectable scruples
           engaging in a lynching. Get me out of this.
           Sally is released by Jones.
JONES   Funny, when I first heard you screaming at the
           rehearsal I didn't think I could manage the ex-
           periment. I suppose you get used to everything.
SALLY   I don't. I can't get used to the barbarity of
           apparently decent human beings. Dr Jones, who
           can you trust?
JONES   There have been people – even in Nazi Ger-
           many, who did obey their own consciences. Not
           many – but there were some. Sooner or later
           one person coming here will refuse to pull down
           the levers.
SALLY   That's the only person I would trust. I think
           I'll have a drink.
JONES   This time of the morning?
SALLY   I need it.

As Sally is taking a swig enter Dr Daly with Harley-Hoare.

JONES   Ah. (*To Sally*) You can go now. Thank you very much.

DALY   Mr Harley-Hoare just wanted to know if you were all right.

SALLY   (*quietly*) You bastard.

HARLEY-H You were so stupid. Why didn't you add up? You didn't even try.

          Exit Sally.

          She didn't even try, did she, Dr Jones?

DALY   Just a few questions.

HARLEY-H Did you hear what she called me? I must say, Dr Daly, you get a funny class of people volunteering to sit in that chair.

JONES   (*wryly*) Ye-es, but then we can't be too choosey.

DALY   First of all we just want to thank you for your co-operation.

HARLEY-H Not at all, doctor. Glad to help. But I must say she was a worthless woman.

DALY   How do you mean?

HARLEY-H Very poor material.

DALY   I expect you hurt her a great deal – inflicted a great deal of pain.

HARLEY-H I only did what Dr Jones asked me to.

JONES   Quite right. Dr Daly, he just obeyed my commands.

DALY   But these shocks were pretty terrific and she did ask you to stop, I gather.

HARLEY-H I think she made a meal of it, you know. Made it sound worse than it was. Of course I realise it must have hurt a bit. I mean you know best about this learning process – I don't understand these things. I admit it got a bit rough at the end, still it was in a good cause, wasn't it?

JONES   Oh yes.

HARLEY-H You devised the experiment.

DALY   Yes, I did.

HARLEY-H   I mean it was your responsibility. I just did as I was told.

JONES   Quite – and you did it well.

HARLEY-H   Thank you. I'm afraid I was a bit green at the beginning, a bit bungling I fear.

JONES   Next time you wouldn't make any mistakes, even little ones.

HARLEY-H   No, no. If you want me to help out again I'm sure I'll be on song, as it were. Ye-es, she put it on a bit, definitely. That sort of woman.

DALY   It was very good of you to come along. Now if we go out to the office we'll pick up that little cheque.

HARLEY-H   Not at all. Only too glad to be of help.

He puts out his hand. Daly hesitates, then shakes hands. They all begin to exit.

I feel extraordinarily hungry. I don't know why.

JONES   Hungry?

HARLEY-H   Famished.

Exit. Lights down.

ACT II

Liz's flat.
Darkness. Spot comes slowly up on Sally asleep
on the divan. As she dreams she is restless. Soon
there is a sound of voices on tape whispering.

KURT   (*on tape whispering*) Add 34,35,36,37,38.

THE REST OF

THE CAST   (*on tape whispering*) 34,35,36,37,38.

KURT   (*on tape louder*) 1,2,3,4,5,6,7,8,9,10.

ALL   (*on tape*) 1,2,3,4,5,6,7,8,9,10.

On the tape now Sally is heard screaming which
is immediately followed by all the rest of
the cast laughing loudly. Sally on the bed
is again restless, and the lights now come up
on the rest of the cast R. stage standing
silently in odd postures giving the whole scene
a sense of unreality, e.g. Daly is in white
coat with his mouth open, his eyes wide, staring.
Suddenly Kurt moves like an automaton towards
Sally on the bed.

DALY   (*calling*) That girl idolises you, Kurt.

GORDON   (*calling*) Kurt!

Kurt, hearing Gordon's voice, stops advancing
towards Sally. Gordon moves towards Kurt in
the same mechanical odd way.

You're wrong. She does not idolise you.

KURT   (*turning towards Gordon*) Well, perhaps.

GORDON   *(threateningly)* Who's wrong?

Now for the rest of the dream scene Daly, Jones, Liz, Nurse and Harley-Hoare act like a kind of Chorus of which Gordon is the dominant and bullying leader. It will be seen from the text that follows that the characters in a way become caricatures of themselves, that a threatening atmosphere pervades Sally's dream, and at the same time, the audience should be allowed to respond to the verbal, surrealistic humour.

KURT   Well . . .

GORDON   What's good for your health?

KURT   Me.

All laugh until Gordon raises his hand.

GORDON   What's good for your health?

KURT   Tomato soup?

GORDON   Celery soup.

KURT   Ye-es, celery soup.

GORDON   Stop weighing yourself all the time!

KURT   Sorry, Gordon, Sorry.

Kurt looks around the theatre.

It's just that there's a fly in here.

LIZ   He's playing dodo.

HARLEY-H   Get his head boiled.

JONES   Get him crossed off the register.

NURSE   Ask him his favourite colour.

KURT   Yellow.

NURSE   His favourite flower.

KURT   Carnations, Gordon; all right, Gordon?

GORDON   What's the best month in the year?

KURT   Please Gordon, for Gawd's sake.

GORDON   The best month in the year?

KURT   December.

GORDON   *(yelling)* September, September, September.

KURT   I meant September.

GORDON   What's good for your health?

KURT   Tomato soup.

GORDON   *(shouting)* Tomato soup?

KURT   I mean celery soup.

GORDON   Wrong. Onion soup. ONION SOUP.

All laugh until Gordon raises his hand to stop them.

KURT   (*to Sally on bed*) I don't like that tune. I hate that tune. So stow it, Sally. I've to practise my speech and you play tunes like that.

GORDON   And the clock's ticking too loud.

NURSE   The roof's leaking.

HARLEY-H   There's a shadow under the table.

DALY   My egg's underdone.

JONES   My toast's burnt.

LIZ   It's nag, nag, nag.

JONES   My toast's black.

ALL   Black, black, black, black.

HARLEY-H   (*in vaudeville voice*) Do you recall a man by the name of Smith?

DALY   Smith? Smith? The name is familiar. Now where did I hear that name.

JONES   No, not Smith. Not Smith. He got electrocuted in the bath. Not Smith.

Gordon laughs silently, hissing. The others pick up the hissing note. All hiss.

LIZ   Gas.

ALL   Gas. Gas. Gas. Gas.

HARLEY-H   Your servant, sir. Your most obedient servant, sir.

DALY   (*pointing at Sally*) Strike her off the books.

HARLEY-H   Expel her from the party.

The 'chorus' now move, their hands to their necks, as if they were drowning.

ALL   Gas. Gas. Gas. Gas. Gas.

Gordon raises his hand commandingly and immediately they stop speaking and moving.

KURT   But I *like* roses.

GORDON   (threateningly) Carnations are better than roses.

KURT   Maybe.

GORDON (*angry*) Maybe?

KURT You're right roses aren't what they're cracked up to be.

GORDON Your favourite colour?

KURT Red.

GORDON I like yellow.

KURT Lot to be said for yellow.

GORDON Yellow's the best.

KURT Lovely colour yellow.

GORDON It's better than lovely.

KURT Yes, yellow's first.

GORDON Better than first.

KURT Yellow's supreme.

GORDON Kurt.

KURT Yellow's the best colour in the world.

HARLEY-H Please don't raise your voice.

DALY No violence please.

NURSE No coughing.

KURT But I liked her in her dark red skirt.

HARLEY-H (*suddenly raising his arms like an orator*) Listen. Listen, I say. (*Screaming*) Listen to my message.

LIZ Speak up.

JONES What's your message?

HARLEY-H Listen.

Harley-Hoare begins to bark like a dog and all laugh.

NURSE The message of the revolutionary party. Where's Enoch? Where the devil is Enoch?

HARLEY-H I'm a celebrity, I really am a celebrity. Right Jack?

DALY Right. Logic. Trust me.

HARLEY-H That'll be all then, you can go now.

NURSE Knock knock, Enoch. Knock Knock, Enoch. Knock Knock Eeeeeee.

ALL Eeeeeeeeeeeeee.

Gordon raises his hand and there is silence.

GORDON Your favourite colour?

KURT   Yellow.

GORDON   Red.

KURT   Red.

GORDON   Blue, I say.

KURT   Blue's my favourite colour.

GORDON   No, black.

KURT   Yes, black, black, black.

GORDON   Your favourite flower?

KURT   Carnations?

GORDON   No.

KURT   Roses.

GORDON   No.

KURT   Black roses?

GORDON   No. Daisies! Daisies! Daisies!

KURT   Black daisies. I love her black daisies.

GORDON   Good boy, now you've got it. The twist of vision. Now you're talking. Now you can see in the dark. Good boy.

Gordon signals to the 'chorus'.

ALL   (*satirically*) Go-od boy.

KURT   (*joyful*) Luminous black daisies. Huge funeral, rain-washed, black daisies.

Gordon slowly claps. Kurt and then 'chorus' all join him in clapping. Kurt rushes to a raised level on the stage.

Where are they working – in the Midlands, in Yorkshire – there they are in the mill, in the factory, in the foundry, in the brick kiln.

HARLEY-H   They are taking our jobs from us.

KURT   All those unpleasant, unskilled jobs.

ALL   Hear, hear.

KURT   The night shifts in the mills, for example, are carried out exclusively by black immigrants.

ALL   Sieg heil, sieg heil, sieg heil.

KURT   This is a fact and many employers in the Midlands and Yorkshire know that their mills, their factories, their foundries and kilns would fold up without such labour.

General hubbub and consternation.
For the white worker has put on his white collar
and journeyed South East.

NURSE   Sieg Heil, Sieg Heil, Sieg –

GORDON Shut up.

KURT   Yes, what is immigrant work? It's unskilled dirty
work, too dirty for white hands.

NURSE   (*turning round and round like a mechanical
doll*) Quisling. White wog. Knock his knockers
off. Knock his knockers off. Knock his knockers
off. Knock his knockers off. Knock his
knockers . . .

GORDON Shut up.

KURT   Next time you wake up in the night and turn
to the wall think of the black man.

DALY   (*chanting*) Insomnia, insomnia. Sodium amytal.

JONES   (*chanting*) Seconal, nembutal, pheno –

GORDON Shut up.

KURT   It's the black man who's working the night shift
when the comfortable whites are always in their
comfortable beds.
General hubbub and consternation.
Tell me, who right now is cleaning the lava-
tories in our government offices or right here
in this hospital?

DALY   Let me answer that.

JONES   Yes, Dr Daly, answer him.

DALY   I'll tell you what science says about that and
about all your problems.
Consternation.

HARLEY-H Quiet for the doctor.

ALL   Give him the floor, give him the floor.

DALY   What I'm trying to tell you, if you'll listen, is
plain – absolutely plain, if you follow my mean-
ing – and if you don't, well don't hesitate to in-
terrupt – for what I'm saying is – is that it's like
a what-do-call-it, honestly.

GORDON That's too high falutin' for me.

G

KURT Too high falutin', you hear what the boss says. Tell us straight.

DALY What I'm telling you, what I've been trying to say is scientific, if you follow me, and I'll only be too happy to explain.
Now speaks so fast that he becomes unintelligible and almost goes berserk. Then the actor should stop adlibbing and continue with –
So just don't nod your head and smile now, as if you understand, and all that crap, for it's a kind of white-washing as a matter of fact.

GORDON Get to the point, get to the point.

KURT You heard him. Get to the scientific point.

HARLEY-H Don't talk to the doctor that way.

DALY *(quickly and wildly)* Thank you. Now to continue what I was saying without in any way trying to inconvenience you and all that, or if you happen to see what I mean in the first place, you would agree, wouldn't you, that it's so damn difficult not to be misunderstood. I mean, if I said blood is vermilion, for Pete's sake, or something like that, I could lead you astray.

JONES We're ready, Dr Daly. We understand. Lead us astray.

DALY First I ought to tell you the recent statistics about what men do after sex.

JONES The American results?

DALY Yes. 28 per cent of American white males after the sexual act turn over and go to sleep, and 12 per cent light up a cigarette.

GORDON What about the others?

DALY Oh the other 60 per cent go home to their wives.
Pause.

NURSE I wear two pairs of knickers.
Long pause.

DALY 34 and 35 and 36 and 37 and 38.

KURT *I'll* pull the lever.

ALL   1,2,3,4,5,6,7,8,9,10.

KURT   Let me pull the lever.

ALL   1,2,3,4,5,6,7,8,9,10.

GORDON   Get her, get her.

All advance towards Sally on the bed.

NURSE   White wog, nigger lover.

KURT   (*chanting*) Pull the black lever. Pull the black lever. Pull the black lever. Trust me. Pull the black lever. Pull the black lever. Pull the black lever.

Now on tape, and as lights dim, all are heard chanting as they exit.

ALL   Trust me. Pull the black lever. Pull the black lever. Pull the black lever. Trust me. Kill the nigger lover. Kill the nigger lover. Kill the nigger lover. Trust us. Kill the nigger lover.

Voices now gradually become whisperings.

Kill the nigger lover. Kill the nigger lover. Trust us.

Doorbell rings.

Lights come up on Sally on bed, otherwise stage empty.

Enter Liz.

LIZ   Sally.

Sally wakes up.

SALLY   What? What?

LIZ   I'd better answer the door. Your boy friend's here already.

SALLY   My God, what time is it?

LIZ   Don't worry. The dinner's almost ready.

Front doorbell rings again.

SALLY   The bell.

LIZ   It's all right. I'll get it.

Exit Liz. Pause.

SALLY   I have a dream.

End of Act

ACT III

Scene One

Scene: The living room in Liz's house as in last scene of Act II. Sally, Kurt and Liz are just finishing dinner. There are empty plates, empty bottles of wine on the table etc.

SALLY   And you really think that by knowing what a man admires you can judge that man?

KURT   It's one indication.

SALLY   Then what do you admire?

KURT   *(rising)* Oh, I dunno. Maybe the brave concealment of a personal tragedy.

SALLY   *(also rising)* I don't think that tells anybody much about you.

KURT   And I admire your cooking too, Liz. That was a great meal.

LIZ   My friend, the American, he admires m-m-me. Can't say that puts him up in my estimation. Or anybody else's.

SALLY   You should have asked him round, Liz.

LIZ   His wife had prior claims.

KURT   You didn't say he was married.

LIZ   There's no point in committing adultery unless you're m-m-married. *(Getting up)* He's so predictable. Every time he decides to make a pass at me he takes his glasses off. His eyes go soft and his right hand reaches for m-m-my left ber-ber-ber-ber ... tit. He's so damn predictable.

SALLY   That's not such a terrible thing – to be predictable I mean.

LIZ   Well, you're predictable sometimes. I know that when you're skint you'll start taking taxis and begin sending telegrams like m-m-mad. And you'll eat in the best restaurants.

SALLY   I don't do that when I can *afford* to get food poisoning.

KURT   That's a typical Sally remark. You *are* afraid of being poisoned.

SALLY   How do you mean?

KURT   In some ways you were being dead serious about food poisoning.

SALLY   You should tell more jokes Kurt.

KURT   No, the danger in that is someone may come back and tell me one. Like I said earlier, we all have to live in perpetual trust. I go into a chip shop, a transport café, or for that matter to the Savoy, and I don't expect to go down with typhoid. I go to the dentist occasionally and I trust him not to drill holes in perfectly good teeth. I have a haircut and I rely on the barber not cut my ears off. But Sally now, she distrusts everybody and everything.

LIZ   You put your car into a garage for servicing and you expect the man to check everything properly. B-brakes, tyres, everything.

KURT   Exactly.

LIZ   You're b-b-bloody crazy!

SALLY   You think I don't trust *you*. That's what you're saying.
Kurt lights a big cigar.

LIZ   I think the devil smokes cigars. If the devil came in right now he'd be wearing evening dress and he'd be smoking a cigar. Very suave is the devil. Wearing a carnation in his lapel and playing the xylophone.

KURT I just think that you're suspicious of the whole human race.

SALLY (*strongly*) I am, I am, I am. So what? Haven't I the right? Napalm, H bombs, concentration camps, private little tortures out of sight, in the dark, in the corners of the world.

LIZ You trust Fidel Castro, Sally.

KURT No, you're just innately suspicious, Sal. Whenever someone says something nice to you, you smell a rat.

SALLY (*smiling*) Not fair.

KURT I think before you'll say you'll marry me and come to the States, I'll have to undergo some holy test. Slay a dragon, kill the devil. Smash his xylophone. Save the fair maiden in her tower.
Sally is no longer smiling and involuntarily she stands up, seems troubled.

LIZ I wish someone would ask me to m-m-m-marry him. He could trust me.

KURT Of course.

LIZ He could trust m-m-me to say yes.

KURT I tell you one thing I admire. Something I've admired, never forgotten. It was a bowl I saw once in Copenhagen. (*Very hesitantly, slowly. Kurt seems happy*) In a museum. A green bowl in a glass. I've never seen such a green. A wonderful green. Green you can't imagine – you just can't imagine. I walked round and round this glass case. It was a green – indescribable. Such a light green, I just stared and stared and then I heard the attendant behind say something. *Kurt seems abstracted now and Liz and Sally are looking at him gently smiling.*
Whatever he said was in Danish. I said I'm from England. Then he spoke in English. Such a wonderful green, I said. It's Ming, he said. Oh, what a green, really you don't know. So

luminous, so ... that light green. Such an indescribable green. (*Pause*) I've never forgotten
that green.

LIZ   Give me a cigar, will you?

KURT   What?

LIZ   Can you spare a cigar?

KURT   Sure. (*Offering cigar*) Are you accustomed to
smoking cigars!

LIZ   I used to all the time before I went to a psychiatrist ... because of my stutter.

KURT   He didn't help?

LIZ   The psychiatrist? No, not much. But I did him
a power of good. (*Lights up*) This will turn me
green. Indescribable green.

SALLY   Know what I did today, Kurt? I took part
in an experiment in a test. I wonder how you
would come out in such a test?

KURT   You slew a dragon?

LIZ   This is be-b-b-better than hash. Have a go at
this, Sal. Join us in our religious rite.

KURT   What was this test then?

SALLY   It doesn't matter.

KURT   Go on.

SALLY   Forget it.

KURT   Now isn't that the most bloody irritating thing?
You start something and –
*Sally goes over to him and suddenly takes his
hand and kisses it.*

LIZ   (*pause*) Oh my God this cigar is b-b-b-big.

SALLY   That's what you did to Gordon, didn't you?

KURT   What?

SALLY   Kiss his hand.

KURT   For crying out loud.

LIZ   Come on, chaps. No quarrelling in front of the
host.

SALLY   Sorry. It's just ... just that I'm tired. I ... this
experiment I took part in today. I feel tired.

KURT   What was it anyway?

LIZ Tell us about it.

SALLY ... well, some time ago they set up an experiment at Yale University – in a psychological laboratory. More than a thousand people participated – and afterwards the whole thing was repeated at several other American Universities. Now a couple of London doctors have devised their own experiment and –

KURT What's the point of it?

SALLY It's just a study of memory and learning in which one person is designated as the teacher and the other as the learner. It's concerned with the effects of what the doctors call negative reinforcement.

LIZ That's as clear as m-m-mud. Crystal clear, isn't it, Kurt?

SALLY The learner is seated in a chair and his arms strapped to stop him moving. Then an electrode is attached to his wrist. He's given a shock every time he makes an error. A mathematical error.

KURT Charming.

SALLY The learner is conditioned to add up correctly and quickly.

LIZ Sounds bonkers to me.

KURT And today you went along as one of those er, teachers?

SALLY Right.

KURT How did you get involved in it?

SALLY Oh, some chap I know asked me if I'd volunteer. They need volunteers badly.

KURT You're just an inveterate do-gooder.

SALLY They're short of people, that's all. It was very interesting as a matter of fact. I said I'd try and find other people to volunteer as teachers.

LIZ OK. Count me in. Sounds b-b-better than giving b-b-blood. Especially *my* ber-ber-ber –

SALLY   No, they want men. They need men very badly, Kurt.

LIZ   M-me too.

SALLY   Pack it in, Liz.

KURT   You want me to volunteer?

SALLY   Well, they're very short of people tomorrow.

KURT   Is it in the daytime?

SALLY   Yeh.

KURT   It's difficult. I've got to be in the office. Besides – well quite honestly – some of these psychological learning tests don't sound very sensible.

SALLY   But I promised, Kurt.

KURT   You promised what?

SALLY   All of us promised. Each one of us said that we would get one other person to come along to the laboratory. Please, Kurt.

KURT   You said something about a test. You said you wondered how I would fare in some sort of test. Is this it?

SALLY   No. I didn't explain it properly. They'll explain it to you. Just let me ring them up and say you'll come tomorrow afternoon.

KURT   Will you be there?

SALLY   No, no. I have to be at the theatre. We have a run through tomorrow. It's an important rehearsal tomorrow.
Pause.

KURT   OK. If you want me to. If you really want me to go along, I will. I suppose I can take the afternoon off.

SALLY   Thank you Kurt.

LIZ   Well, how about some coffee?

SALLY   I'll make it.

LIZ   No, I'll do it.
You made the dinner. Kurt and I will fix it. You take it easy, put your feet up.
Sally takes Kurt's hand and they begin to exit to kitchen.

LIZ   You don't need two people to put the kettle on.

SALLY   We do, love. Me to turn the gas on and Kurt to strike a match.
Kurt and Sally embrace.

LIZ   I have the distinct feeling you two want me to be alone.

SALLY   By the way, Kurt, when you go along to the laboratory, I'd rather you didn't mention my name.

KURT   Why ever not?
Exit Kurt and Sally. Liz picks up a journal, looks fed up. Lights gradually come down to darkness.

ACT III

The laboratory

*When lights rise again we are in Mr Harley-
Hoare's office.*
*Harley-Hoare is banging successive papers with
rubber stamp when Kurt enters.*

KURT   Busy?

HARLEY-H   Just giving these the old rubber stamp.

KURT   I'm going off to Dr Daly's laboratory this afternoon.
Harley-Hoare suddenly stops.
I understand you've been. My secretary told
me.

HARLEY-H   It was confidential.

KURT   Oh, I'm sorry. She didn't even tell me con-
fidentially.
Harley-Hoare resumes rubber stamping.
It doesn't matter me knowing, does it? I mean
I'm volunteering myself and I'm not keeping it
a secret. I have to go shortly, and I'm curious
to know how you made out.

HARLEY-H   A.1. Very well. Definitely. Yes, it was a chal-
lenge.

KURT   Can't you get one of the younger clerks to do
that?

HARLEY-H   You can't trust the youngsters these days. You
have to do everything yourself.

KURT   Still they couldn't go far wrong with that could
they?

HARLEY-H   (*momentarily stops banging*) They could get it upside down, sir. (*Continues stamping*) They're just clock watchers nowadays. They just come into the office to let their hair grow. Very poor material.

KURT   I gather that one has to pull down different levers which give the student a shock when he makes a mistake.

HARLEY-H   Student?

KURT   They are students, aren't they?

HARLEY-H   The one I had didn't exactly look like a student. A strident bag, she was. Still these days ... students! Some of them, the way they behave, deserve a few shocks. Too clever by half, some of them, with Trotsky this and Ché that.

KURT   Well, students ought to be bright.

HARLEY-H   Quite right, sir.

KURT   And one expects them to be rebellious and to be concerned with moral issues.

HARLEY-H   Oh yes, I have a great respect for students.
Enter Gordon. Immediately Harley-Hoare bangs the papers at an increased rate.

GORDON   Ah Kurt, there you are. I want you to come to the conference at 4.

KURT   Can't. Sorry, Gordon.

GORDON   What?

KURT   I've promised to be elsewhere.

GORDON   (*to Harley-Hoare*) What are you doing?

HARLEY-H   Pardon?

GORDON   What the hell are you up to?

HARLEY-H   I'll be through with this in a tick, sir.
Harley-Hoare is now banging papers at an incredible rate.

GORDON   Stop it. STOP IT.

HARLEY-H   Beg your pardon, but I –

GORDON   Now Kurt, what's this about not coming to the conference?

KURT   I've promised to go to the hospital.

HARLEY-H   To see Dr Daly. He's volunteered for the experiment.

GORDON   *You?*

KURT   Yes, why not? Do you know about Dr Daly's set up?

GORDON   Who suggested *you* should volunteer?

KURT   Sally Parsons. Why?
Gordon suddenly laughs silently.

GORDON   That's a good one. Ha, ha, ha.

KURT   What's funny?

GORDON   Sally Parsons suggested you should volunteer to give her electric shocks. Ha, ha, ha. That's rich, that's gravy rich. Kinky. Ha, ha, ha. She should talk about others being kinky. Ha, ha, ha.

KURT   What's the big joke? She volunteered to pull down the levers. Now I am.

GORDON   Ha, ha, ha. It's very funny.

HARLEY-H   Ha, ha, ha. It is funny. It's very funny, isn't it sir? Ha, ha, ha.

GORDON   (*stops laughing*) What is?

HARLEY-H   That we should all . . . well . . . happen to volunteer.

GORDON   Your girl friend never volunteered, Kurt. She'll be sitting in the chair. She wants you to shock her to hell, don't you see? She's testing you out. Testing to see whether you'll be brute enough to give her maximum shocks like this, this runt did probably.

HARLEY-H   Brute enough? *Brute enough?*

KURT   I don't understand.

HARLEY-H   Who is this Sally Parsons? Was she the woman in the chair?

GORDON   That's right. The lady in the chair – I'll spell it out for you – was sweet little, kinky little Sally bloody Parsons, ha ha, ha. She's a good friend of Mr Jennings here. A very good friend, and by profession an actress. And you thought you gave her shocks. Only you didn't.

HARLEY-H I gave her shocks all right, oh brother I gave her shocks. She was screaming. I'm telling you she raised the roof. She was no friend of Mr Jennings. I'm sure of that. She wasn't ... no, no, the type.

GORDON It wasn't really wired up, you pretentious git. You pulled down the levers and she screamed very convincingly, that's all. She's an actress, Mr Harley-Hoare, an actress. And no doubt she can scream like any good woman.

HARLEY-H An actress?

KURT It's absurd Gordon. What the hell are you suggesting? Sally knows I wouldn't give her shocks.

HARLEY-H It's to do with the learning process, Dr Daly told me.

KURT Yes, with conditioning – Sally said so. It's a psychological learning test.

GORDON (to Harley-Hoare) Yes, they are learning how men like you will obey commands however evil, they are confirming that ordinary citizens like you will destroy people if they see it as a duty and if they are ordered to do so by some higher authority.

HARLEY-H (loudly) What is this?

KURT (louder) What's the learning process to do with acting? Or with Sally?

GORDON Don't you understand yet?

HARLEY-H That middle-aged woman in the chair was no actress. I can tell an actress from a ... listen I'm no baby in nappies when it comes to actresses.

KURT You're lying Gordon. What game are you playing?

GORDON Ha, ha, ha.

HARLEY-H When I was in the RAF. I was on the entertainments committee at my last station. They sent these troupers round. Real troupers. At

the camp cinema there was a bit of a stage
and in the spotlight they'd bash out their acts,
singing the old songs for the boys, Paper Doll,
Starlight.

KURT   Just a minute.

HARLEY-H   Smoke gets in your Eyes, Sophisticated Lady.

KURT   (loud) Just a second.

HARLEY-H   Can't get Indiana off my mind. Very accomp-
lished.

KURT   You said it was a middle-aged lady in the chair?

HARLEY-H   As a matter of fact I dealt with these people
personally. I can tell an actress from a . . .

GORDON   Human being? Ha, ha, ha.

KURT   Middle-aged, Gordon. The lady in the chair
was middle-aged.

GORDON   Ha, ha, ha.

KURT   Are you trying to suggest I wouldn't recognise
her, that Sally is so made up that – (Shakes
his head, baffled)

HARLEY-H   With a wig? Are you telling me it's a wig?

GORDON   That's what I'm telling you both.

HARLEY-H   (loud) But you fixed it for me. You spoke to
Dr Daly on my behalf. You cheated . . . You
rotten swi . . .

GORDON   Yes?

HARLEY-H   That woman. This Sally Parsons. She doesn't
deserve a Christian burial.

KURT   Go to hell, Gordon. GO TO HELL.

GORDON   Actresses, you see. One minute they're Virgin
Queens in great marble palaces and the next
they're penniless poxed whores in a doss house.
Well, that's great. But in between times, Kurt,
they're nothing. They have no identity at all.
You want to marry a woman like that Kurt?
You want to marry someone who wants to make
quite sure you are not an incipient Nazi before
she signs on the dotted line?

Suddenly Harley-Hoare picks up rubber stamp

and bangs at the papers. Kurt and Gordon stare at him, then Kurt turns on his heel and exits.

(*Calling*) Kurt. It's for the best, Kurt. (*Pause*) Yes, it's a stroke of luck. Do stop banging away. (*Pause*) Please. Oh, come on, Mr Harley-Hoare, stop sulking.

Harley-Hoare stops.

HARLEY-H   I'm bitterly disappointed.

GORDON   What about?

HARLEY-H   It's not fair, sir.

GORDON   But I'm pleased with you.

HARLEY-H   Pleased?

GORDON   Sure I am. Give me a cigarette, will you? I left mine on my desk.

HARLEY-H   You misled me. You do owe me an apology.

GORDON   Oh, I see. You want to resign?

HARLEY-H   Resign? Well . . . I hadn't thought.

GORDON   Do think, do think.

Harley-Hoare brings out his cigarettes and tentatively offers Gordon one. Gordon smiles, takes one.

So you want your cards? Have you a light?

HARLEY-H   I've worked here a long time, Mr Gordon. But really, I don't know what to say. *An actress.*

GORDON   I'd appreciate it if you didn't tell anybody that Dr Daly is using an actress. You see, it's a medical secret.

HARLEY-H   Oh quite. You can depend on me sir. All the same you took me in and I feel . . . misused.

GORDON   I couldn't tell you, don't you see? I mean medical confidences have to be kept.

HARLEY-H   I respect that but . . .

GORDON   So I hardly owe you an apology.

HARLEY-H   On the other hand.

GORDON   You still think that I have malignantly misled you?

HARLEY-H   I wouldn't say that.

GORDON   You think the worst of me?

HARLEY-H   No, no, sir, no.

GORDON   You thought the worst of me?

HARLEY-H   Of course not.

GORDON   You did.

HARLEY-H   If you think I thought that, well, I'm very sorry. I'm very sorry I gave you that impression, sir.

GORDON   Are you apologising to me then?

HARLEY-H   Certainly. It was very wrong of me to jump to conclusions. I do apologise. Medical confidential, quite.

GORDON   But you still want your cards?
Harley-Hoare suddenly leaps forward with a light for Gordon's cigarette.
Thank you.

HARLEY-H   No, no, under the circumstances I'd be grateful if ... I don't want my cards, no no. Why should I? You accept my apology, sir?

GORDON   So you don't want your cards?

HARLEY-H   No.

GORDON   But you want a rise?

HARLEY-H   A rise? No, no. A rise, heavens no.

GORDON   Ha, ha, ha. I'm pleased with you. Ha, ha, ha. I'm pleased with everything. Why shouldn't you have your rise?

HARLEY-H   I'm pleased if you're pleased.

GORDON   Things have worked out very well. Everything is going to be very good.

HARLEY-H   Excellent.

GORDON   This will put the tin hat on it.

HARLEY-H   Absolutely. (*Pause*) On what, sir?

GORDON   It's great.

HARLEY-H   Quite, I was going to say that ... it's a great .... day.

GORDON   You're happy here.

HARLEY-H   Yes sir. You're happy sir? (*Pause*) You said something about a rise.

GORDON   Don't you think I should give you a rise?

H

HARLEY-H   If you think you should, I think you should.

GORDON   But don't you feel guilty?

HARLEY-H   I have apologised, sir.

GORDON   I don't mean contrition. I mean guilt.

HARLEY-H   I don't quite follow you.

GORDON   You want justice.

HARLEY-H   *You* . . . I can rely on you, I'm sure.

GORDON   Then you do feel guilty.

HARLEY-H   Only generally.

GORDON   Sure, sure, generally. Like when you have refused a beggar alms.

HARLEY-H   (*puzzled*) I suppose so.

GORDON   Yes, I understand. It's true for all of us. Afterwards we worry ourselves for a minute or two. Feel guilt. Then perhaps we reassure ourselves. Tell ourselves, *well* he was a professional beggar anyway. He would have drunk up the value of the silver coin we turned over in our pockets.

HARLEY-H   That's it. I know that feeling.

GORDON   You do understand. You're sweating Mr Harley-Hoare.

HARLEY-H   It's warm in here.

GORDON   It's like when you turn off the television set when they are about to show you once again the atrocities in Africa or Asia, turn off the images of starving children, the children with Belsen eyes. You don't want to see that any more so you turn the set off, right? And you feel guilty for turning the set off. Why are you sweating?

HARLEY-H   It *is* warm in here. Very warm. I try and do my duty sir.

GORDON   You shall have justice. I'm going to raise your salary by 4 per cent. Don't you think I should?

HARLEY-H   You know best sir.

GORDON   *It's not enough.* How about 8 per cent?

HARLEY-H   That's very generous.

GORDON   You're pleased then? Ha, ha. Ha, ha, ha.

HARLEY-H You won't regret it.

GORDON No siree, I won't. You know Harley-Hoare . . . I've done two good deeds today. I've stopped a boy making a disastrous marriage. That's worth doing, is it not? That gives me satisfaction. One day Kurt will thank me and see that my motives were pure – which they are. Yet I wonder if he'll ever believe me. She's psychologically a bad bet. Oh yes, I know all about her. I can feel pity for her. But I don't want her to marry anyone I'm fond of. I don't want Kurt crucified.

HARLEY-H And the second good thing is that you have raised my salary.

GORDON That's right. At least I've made you a slightly happier man.

HARLEY-H That's true, and I'm grateful.

GORDON You're an odd man, Harley-Hoare.

HARLEY-H Me, odd? I don't think *I'm* odd.

GORDON Well, perhaps not. It's simply that you renew my belief in the unfathomable strangeness of every human being.

Gordon waves and exits and Harley-Hoare returns to stamping papers. After a while he stops and looks at the audience with a delighted aspect of glee on his face as lights dim for the next scene in the laboratory.

ACT III

The Laboratory Lights come up on Sally and Dr Jones.

JONES I just can't allow this, you just can't manipulate our experiments in this personal way. I just have to tell Dr Daly.

SALLY It's too late now. Dr Daly would be furious. Kurt would be furious.

JONES They both have a right to be.

SALLY In five minutes he'll be in here. In half an hour he will go again. No one need ever know. Kurt won't recognise me and Dr Daly will have one more statistic to add to his list. So no harm will be done. *Please.* (*Takes whisky flask out of her bag*) Holy Lenin, I'm sorry I told you.

JONES I tell you as a doctor – if you don't watch it you'll end up in the chronic alcoholic ward. It's just another way of committing suicide slowly.

SALLY Better than drugs, isn't it?

JONES I'm not so sure. It may be better to be hooked on opium than alcohol. I'm not a fanatical tee-totaller so listen to me. As one wise man put it, the difference between the alcoholic and the drug addict, is this: the alcoholic becomes high, returns home and beats his wife; the drug addict becomes high, returns home and his wife beats him.

SALLY Look Olwen, let me have a chance of getting married first, I can worry about the beatings afterwards.

JONES But do you want to marry this fellow? It doesn't

116

sound like it to me.

SALLY Please don't moralise again.

JONES The way you've got him here with all your...
pretences – to test him out for heaven's sake.
It would be best if you went out there now,
even at this late hour, and owned up.

SALLY There's one thing I haven't told you before...
I haven't told anybody.

JONES Well?

SALLY I think I'm pregnant.

JONES You're lying.

SALLY I'm not.

JONES You are. And even if you're not, then all the
more reason to stop this charade.

SALLY You're like my mother.

JONES What?

SALLY You're as hard as nails.

JONES I'm not your mother and I'm not hard as nails.

SALLY *And I'm not lying.*

JONES I can only give you advice. That's all a doctor
can do.

SALLY You don't know anything. I bet you're still a
virgin. I can imagine you 20 years ago in a
panic as a little amorous scuffle developed on
some medical student's divan.
Jones coldly turns and makes as if to exit.
Don't tell them. I told you in confidence and
you're a doctor. You're not a priest and you
can't give me absolution but I confessed to you,
and you have no right to go sneaking off and
telling –

JONES (*loud*) Sally! (*Quietly*) I won't tell anybody
– but I can't have any part in this. It's a deception and I'm opting out of it. Dr Daly can call
out the numbers himself. Tomorrow I suggest
we have a talk. You and I need to talk.

SALLY You don't like me do you?

JONES Don't be daft. Frankly I feel sorry for you.

SALLY   Thanks. Ta. (*Pause*) I hate myself. (*Goes to chair and sits in it*) Will you strap me in, at least?
Jones straps Sally in the chair.

JONES   I hope it works out for you. I hope your young man comes through with *flying* colours, see. If he does, it's more than you deserve though.

SALLY   I'm not even sure that I want him to come through with, as you put it, *flying* colours. (*Tortured*) I don't know what I want. I don't know, I don't know, I don't know.

JONES   You said you hated yourself. I believe you. But you ought to know that as self-hatred grows the ability to really love anybody dies.

SALLY   Ha. Bully for you, Dr Jones.
Pause

JONES   Dew, you're just a child. That assumed toughness doesn't fool anyone. Tell Dr Daly I was called away and won't be back until tomorrow.
Exit Dr Jones. Sally in chair after a short while closes her eyes. Soon there are voices off.

DALY   (*off*) No, no, nurse, you needn't bother. If you'll take these forms back to the office. Thank you. This way, Mr Jennings.

KURT   (*off*) And it goes up you say in increments of 40 volts.

DALY   (*off*) Correct. Ah, in here, Mr Jennings – after you.
Enter Kurt and Dr Daly.
This is our other volunteer. All ready, I see. Good.
Kurt keeps his distance from Sally. They just nod at each other.
And here are the levers. Would you care to inspect them Mr Jennings?
While Kurt looks at levers Daly talks quietly to Sally.

DALY   Where's Dr Jones?

SALLY   She was called away. She won't be in until to-morrow.

DALY   Oh. Everything clear, Mr Jennings?

KURT   Very clear. And now you intend to make her add up various sums, is that right?

DALY   Uh-huh.

KURT   And I'm to throw these levers and give her electric shocks if she makes errors.

DALY   Quite right.

KURT   At a certain point it will cause a great deal of pain. I mean if she makes many mistakes.

DALY   Yes, she knows that.

KURT   And she doesn't mind?

DALY   No. For this she has freely volunteered.

KURT   (*to Sally*) You don't mind receiving even high electric shocks if you make mistakes?
Sally shakes her head.
(*To Daly*) I know scientists have trained rats to perform all kinds of rat miracles by giving them shocks.

DALY   Quite. Shall we start?
Daly turns all lights down so that Sally is now in a white spotlight.

KURT   But rats aren't human beings.

DALY   Of course not. The same with drugs. Drugs are tried out on laboratory animals and all kinds of tests are conducted. There comes a time though when the laboratory animal tests have to be carried out on human beings. Medical progress can only work this way.

KURT   No. Rats aren't human beings. Rats can't volunteer to take part in such experiments.

DALY   (*jovially*) No, that's true. Well now – all set?

KURT   I must tell you, Dr Daly, I don't like this experiment.

DALY   Oh, but you did volunteer. Of course, if you would rather not go on with it at this late stage, then you are free to withdraw. However, I hope you will not let us down. After all, we haven't started yet. (*To Sally*) You are ready, aren't you?

Sally nods affirmatively.

KURT   You really want to go on with this?

Sally just smiles.

DALY   Yes, she does. Now Mr Jennings, if you have any more questions I would rather you addressed them to me.

KURT   You have explained that the reason for this experiment is to discover the relationship between punishment and the learning process – well that reason does seem laudable.

DALY   Quite. Are you ready then to start?

KURT   But it's such a thing, such a thing, such a thing!

DALY   What?

Kurt turns away, his back to Dr Daly and Sally.

DALY   I really must insist either you refuse definitely to participate in this experiment or we start at once. We only have a limited time at our disposal, you see.

No reply from Kurt.

Do I understand that you won't participate in our experiment?

KURT   (*turning*) Why not?

DALY   Very well.

KURT   Why should I back out now? I haven't changed my mind. Nor has she changed her mind.

DALY   Then please go to the white lever.

KURT   The first one?

DALY   Yes.

KURT   And this white lever, that's the first one I pull down?

DALY   Yes.

KURT   This red lever is the last one?

DALY   Yes, the red lever is the last. But as I told

you – if you pull down the red lever consecutively it will increase the voltage even more than just pulling it once.

KURT   That could be dangerous.

DALY   It has its dangers. Our subject here understands that.

KURT   So I just pull it down (*screaming*) LIKE THIS.

Kurt pulls down the red lever consecutively and the red light goes on and off and on and off and on and off. We see Sally's face change from surprise to silent tears. She does not make a sound. Daly puts both arms in the air and for a moment is dumbstruck.

DALY   (*shouting*) Stop it. STOP IT.
Daly makes to put all lights on.
Kurt comes away from the levers.
You're crazy, you're really crazy.

KURT   You idiot. Don't you think I knew that this is one goddam, bloody hoax? Who the hell do you think you are?

SALLY Kurt!

KURT   For God's sake you – *you* shut up. I tell you something, Sally, you're fouled up. You're a case and you need help.

DALY   I don't understand. I mean – you called her Sally. You know her?

KURT   Yes, I know her. I know her too damn well.

DALY   Now look here –

KURT   No. You look here. Fraud is not research. You wanted me to be one of your victims, you wanted to luxuriate in the pleasure of your own personal power. With the excuse that it's for the fatherland. The fatherland of Science.

DALY   Now, come, you misunderstand. What we are doing is part of a scientific enquiry. Sally knows that even if you don't.

SALLY   (*quietly*) I hate you. I hate you all. I feel so depressed. I don't know what's wrong with me. Everybody's voices are just *too loud*.
Sally closes her eyes.

KURT   I question the moral basis of your so-called experiment. Why, you're using people like me as guinea pigs and they don't even know. You *fool* them.

DALY   You're confused. Are you all right Sally?

KURT   I'm not confused. This experiment is like a practical joke. Indeed, like a practical joker you play tricks on your victims. You reduce them to fools and in so doing you assert your own power.

DALY   I'm not going to argue with you. You don't understand the mind of a scientist. He is motivated by curiosity. True, curiosity leads to knowledge and knowledge to power. But we are all threatened by our own ignorance – and it is more than power we are after. It's a sense of security that we need. For not much is visible, and not often, do you understand? The world is at war with itself because man is at war with himself. And he needs help. We all need help. Why do you think that I am a doctor?

KURT   I understand that you don't understand your own motives. But then nor do I. (*Aggressive*) Heaven knows what sort of extraordinary unconscious gratification you are getting out of these practical jokes. It's a big laugh, really, you finally fool yourself . . .

DALY   I can't talk to you.
Daly turns on his heel and begins to exit.

KURT   You don't want to hear the truth. Every person who pulls down the levers is *your victim*.
Exit Daly.

SALLY   Let me go, Kurt.

KURT   You! (*Pause*) You should have trusted me.

SALLY   Undo these straps, please.

KURT   You put me on trial.

SALLY   I know. I'm sorry.

KURT   You're a bitch, you know that? You're a bitch in London and you'd be a bitch in New York.

SALLY   I said I'm sorry. I know it was wrong, I'm sorry. I said I'm sorry, I can't say any more than sorry.

KURT   And if I hadn't recognised you, or if I hadn't known it was you in that chair, would you still have been sorry? (*Pause*) You're abrasive and difficult and sometimes you cry out like ... I dunno ... like an animal that's not *well*. But *this* I can't take.

SALLY   Undo the straps please. Let me get out of this chair. Don't just accuse me in this chair. Look, it's not so terrible. I haven't committed a great crime.
        Kurt goes towards her tentatively as if to release her.

KURT   You don't really care for me at all.

SALLY   I do, I do, John.
        Kurt turns away as if he'd received a blow.

KURT   John?

SALLY   Oh my God.

KURT   You can't do more than apologise. That's it, you can't. That's reasonable.

SALLY   We could begin again, Kurt.

KURT   So now you are calling me Kurt.
        Kurt begins to exit.

SALLY   Kurt!

KURT   You *can't*.
        Exit Kurt.

SALLY   For pity's sake, Kurt. I'm sorry.
        Pause as she struggles to get out of the chair and calls:

I do need help, Kurt.
She struggles again with the straps.
Kurt! Dr Daly! Dr Daly! Help, help! Oh
hell. Dr Daly! Kurt! Help! Help! HELP!
*Lights go down and Sally looks upwards at
fading spot and speaks quietly.*
Oh God, help. (*Pause*) I wanna die. Oh God.
Pull the black lever, I wanna die.

Response II

Dear Dannie Abse,

Now that I have read your play, I am in a better position to comment on it. First, the play, as you correctly state in your introduction, took my experiment as a point of departure, but the experiment as portrayed on the stage is not the experiment conducted in my laboratory. It is an imaginative extension of this work. By the same token, the inevitable dramatic judgment made in the play is applicable only to the version of the experiment you have created, and I would surely not wish my experiments judged on the basis of your theatrical rendering of it. Those interested in a serious, ethical examination of my experiment may wish to follow up several of the references I append to this letter.

Your play deals with victimization, and concludes with the view that the true victim of the obedience experiment is the experimental participant. The attempt to equate the experimental victim with the subject is, at best, superficial. The victim in my experiment, strapped into a chair, is exposed to depredations beyond his control. But the naïve subject is a free moral agent who can halt the experiment by the exercise of his own will. The obedience experiment is not a study in which the subject is treated as a passive object, acted upon without any possibility of controlling his own experience. Indeed, the entire experimental situation has been created to allow the subject to exercise a human choice, and thus express his nature as a person. The crux of the experiment, and perhaps its power, lies in the fact that it allows the participant to express a moral choice.

Issues of deception and the experience of tension never

126

in themselves can constitute a final judgment on the experiment; only the participant knows whether deception had the character of a demeaning experience or is as cheerfully forgiven as the misinformation that takes him to a surprise party. My experiments could proceed on a moral basis because I was continually informed by subjects of their acceptability. And this is the central fact that distinguishes my experiment from the dramatized event you have presented.

Your character, Kurt, asserts that the subjects in the experiment are victimized, and this may well be true of the 'experiment', as presented on stage. But is this true in real life? Consider the letter, cited earlier, from a subject who became a conscientious objector. You may not think it is important that through participation in the study, the subject learned something about the dangers of indiscriminate submission to authority. I disagree. He was going to be sent by our government to Southeast Asia to drop napalm on innocent villagers, to despoil the land, to massacre. He informs me, as many others have done, that the experiment has deepened his understanding of the moral problems of submitting to malevolent authority. He has learned something. He takes a stand. He becomes a conscientious objector. Has he been victimized by the experiment, or has he been liberated by it?

Sincerely
Stanley Milgram
Professor

REFERENCES

Milgram, Stanley. Some Conditions of Obedience and Disobedience to Authority. *Human Relations,* 1965, 18: 57–76.

Baumrind, Diana. Some Thoughts on Ethics of Research: After Reading Milgram's 'Behavioral Study of Obedience.' *American Psychologist,* 1964, 19: 421–423.

Milgram, Stanley. Issues in the Study of Obedience: A Reply to Baumrind. *American Psychologist,* 1964, 19: 848–852.

Kelman, Herbert C. Human Use of Human Subjects: The Problem of Deception in Social Psychological Experiments. *Psychological Bulletin,* 1967, 67: 1–11.

Crawford, Thomas J. In Defense of Obedience Research: An Extension of the Kelman Ethic.

All of the above are reprinted in a thoughtful anthology: *The Social Psychology of Psychological Research.* Arthur G. Miller (Editor), New York: The Free Press; London: Collier-Macmillan Ltd. 1972.

Elms, Alan C. *Social Psychology & Social Relevance* Boston: Little Brown & Company 1972.